Vadims Kolmogorovs

Logistics Outsourcing

Vadims Kolmogorovs

Logistics Outsourcing

A way to increase efficiency

VDM Verlag Dr. Müller

Bibliografische Information der Deutschen Nationalbibliothek:
Die Deutsche Nationalbibliothek verzeichnet diese Publikation in der Deutschen Nationalbibliografie; detaillierte bibliografische Daten sind im Internet über http://dnb.d-nb.de abrufbar.

Kontakt: info@vdm-buchverlag.de
Coverbild: www.PureStockX.com
Covererstellung:bd

Herstellung: Schaltungsdienst Lange o.H.G.,
Zehrensdorfer Str. 11, D-12277 Berlin

ISBN: 978-3-8364-0554-6

Table of Contents

Table of Contents .... **II**
List of Abbreviations .... **IV**
List of Tables and Figures .... **V**

Introduction **6**
1. Theoretical background **9**
1.1 The concept of core competence as a basis for outsourcing 9
1.1.1 Identifying core competencies 11
1.2 Outsourcing and supply chain management: common trends 12
1.2.1 Reduction of vertical integration and short term focus 12
1.2.2 Avoidance of high capital investments 14
1.2.3 SCM as core competence 15
1.2.4 Cooperation management 16
2. Defining Supply Chain Management **18**
2.1 Definitions 18
2.2 SCM perspectives with particular reference to outsourcing 20
2.2.1 Applications outsourcing 21
2.2.2 Forth Party Logistics 21
2.2.3 Third Party Logistics 23
3. Logistics Outsourcing **24**
3.1 Initial point 24
3.2 Logistics functions and its outsourcing potential 26
3.2.1 Transportation 29
3.2.2 Warehousing 30
3.2.3 Shipment consolidation 31
3.2.4 Freight Forwarding 32
3.2.5 Invoice audit 34

4. Benefits and potential pitfalls of outsourcing **35**
4.1 Benefits of outsourcing 35
4.1.1 Cost reduction 36
4.1.2 Avoidance of major investments 37
4.1.3 Wider skills pool 38
4.1.4 Quality of service 38
4.1.5 Higher flexibility 39
4.1.6 Improved ratios 39
4.1.7 Transformation of fixed costs into variable costs 40
4.1.8 Reduction of capital commitment 40
4.2 Potential pitfalls of outsourcing 41
4.2.1 Poor or non-performance 43
4.2.2 Loss of logistics know-how 43
4.2.3 Start up difficulties 44
4.2.4 Loss of motivation 44
4.2.5 Business transition and social plan 45
4.2.6 Dependency on the vendor 46
5. Planning Stage **47**
5.1 Outsourcing Forms 47
5.2 Identifying potential providers 50
5.3 Request for proposal 53
5.4 Selecting the vendor 55
5.4.1 Evaluation criteria 56
5.4.2 Establishing a scoring system 56
5.4.3 Weighting the key criteria 57
5.4.4 Making final selection 57
Conclusion **59**
List of References **61**
Bibliography **68**
Appendices **70**

List of Abbreviations

BGL	Bundesverband Güterkraftverkehr Logistik und Entsorgung e.V.
BME	Bundesverband Materialwirtschaft, Einkauf und Logistik e.V.
BPO	Business Process Outsourcing
BVL	Bundesvereinigung Logistik e.V.
BVT	Bundesverband der Transportunternehmen e.V.
CLM	Council of Logistics Management
CPG	Consumer Packaged Goods
DSLV	Deutschen Speditions- und Logistikverband e.V.
DVZ	Deutscher Verkehrs-Verlag
GDP	Gross Domestic Product
HBR	Harvard Business Review
HP	Hewlett Packard
IT	Information Technology
IWIM	Institut für Weltwirtschaft und Internationales Management
JIT	Just-in-Time
PC	Personal Computer
ROI	Return on Investment
ROS	Return on Sales
SC	Supply Chain
SCM	Supply Chain Management
WMS	Warehouse Management System
2PL	Second Party Logistics
3PL	Third Party Logistics
4PL	Fourth Party Logistics

List of Tables and Figures

Diagram 1: Reduction of Vertical Integration...13

Diagram 2: The SCM perspectives 20

Diagram 3: European Market for Fourth Party Logistics 22

Diagram 4: Outsourcing volume in Europe 24

Diagram 5: Forecasted outsourcing volume in Germany 25

Diagram 6: Different kinds of logistics outsourcing activities..............................26

Diagram 7: Determination of outsourcing potential 27

Diagram 8: Top 10 Outsourcing Functions..28

Diagram 9: Benefits of Outsourcing from managers' point of view.....................36

Diagram 10: Failure factors in logistics outsourcing...42

Diagram 11: Evaluation criteria for outsourcing vendor selection 57

Introduction

Supply Chain Management (SCM) is a management concept aimed at organising and optimising the complete value chain from sourcing raw materials to the final customer regardless of organisational boundaries[1]. In recent years, the strategy of concentrating on core competencies of companies led to a vertical disintegration of processes along the value chain[2]. Practical experience shows that companies focusing on their core competencies in first turn outsource logistics operations within their supply chain to external service providers[3].

Outsourcing is defined as "the practice of buying goods and services from outside suppliers, rather than producing them within a firm."[4] *Harvard Business Review* (HBR), the popular management journal recently listed outsourcing as one of the most influential concepts coined in the last 75 years[5].

A fundamental question to ask in this work is whether outsourcing is really value enhancing and, in particular, whether the firm that undertakes outsourcing becomes more efficient[6] as a result. In the context of this work the degree of efficiency will be addressed by analysing the input side as labour costs and capital for initial investments[7].

It will be shown that in an attempt to increase efficiency by reducing expenses and turning fixed costs into variable costs, companies pursue restructuring procedures that include outsourcing of non-core activities to specialists having a

---

[1] cf. Handfield, R. B. & Nichols, E. L. (1999). Introduction to Supply Chain Management. Upper Saddle River: Prentice Hall. p. 2 as cited by Seuring, S. & Goldbach, M. (eds). (2002). Cost Management in Supply Chains. Heidelberg: Physica-Verlag. p. 17

[2] cf. ibid.

[3] cf. Schary, P. B. & Skjott-Larsen, T. (2001). Managing the Global Supply Chain, 2nd Edition. Copenhagen: Copenhagen Business School Press. p. 226

[4] Black, J. (2003). A Dictionary of Economics (2nd ed). Oxford: Oxford University Press. p. 337

[5] cf. Jayasimha, K. R. (2002). Logistics Management – An Introduction. Retrieved on-line in the Internet on the 21st of April 2006: http://www.icfaipress.org/books/Logistics%20management%20-%20Vol-1.asp. p. 1

[6] Efficiency – the degree to which inputs are used in relation to a given level of outputs. Managers judge the degree of efficiency by comparing actual outputs achieved with actual inputs (such as the costs of material and labour). Source: Horngren, C. T. et. al. (2005). Introduction to management accounting, 14th ed. Upper Saddle River: Pearson/Prentice Hall. p. 317

[7] cf. Horngren, C. T. et. al. ibid.

lower cost base due to better economies of scale and scope[8]. In addition, efficiency may also be improved because adjusting output to variations in demand and maintaining the quality of inputs may be easier via enforcing contracts with outside suppliers than in dealing with a strongly unionized internal workforce[9].

However, according to Porter, increase in production efficiency alone will not lead to the long-term competitive advantage as there is a risk that the main innovative achievements and know-how can be copied by competitors[10]. Concentration on core competencies and its protection is considered to be enormously important in sustaining the on-going growth. Therefore, this work is also intended to explain the importance of core competencies and to give an insight into the identification of capabilities which are considered to be core (Chapter 1). In order to underline the role of outsourcing in SCM and to prove that concentration on core competencies found confirmation in practice, common trends in development of both concepts are analysed in this part of the work.

Chapter 2 provides definitions of SCM and logistics and narrows the scope of investigation. Different perspectives of SCM are derived from the concept giving appropriate examples of corresponding outsourcing issues. As in most companies, the logistics function is not seen as a core competence (strategic reason) and since it requires a high level of capital commitment which is not preferred by business practitioners (financial reason), the main emphasis of this work is placed on the logistics perspective.

Each logistics activity represents a certain level of competence in a company. If this level is low and competence is not considered to be core, then the issue of outsourcing as a possible means for improving efficiency is raised. Therefore, Chapter 3 is dedicated to different logistics functions and their outsourcing

---

[8] cf. Financing the Supply Chain. (2001), in Lloyd's Shipping Economist, November 2001. pp. 23-26

[9] cf. Black, J. loc. cit. p. 337

[10] cf. Porter, M. (1999). Wettbewerb und Strategie. München: Econ. pp. 51-52 as cited by Müller-Dauppert, B. (ed). (2005). Logistik-Outsourcing: Ausschreibung, Vergabe, Controlling. München: Verlag Heinrich Vogel. p.11

potential. The most fundamental logistics functions that are outsourced in practice are discussed here in detail.

In order to determine the degree to which logistics operations are successfully outsourced and to find out what the related risks are, a detailed discussion on the most significant benefits and potential pitfalls is given in Chapter 4. Here, the notion of efficiency is addressed directly by examining such benefits of outsourcing as a cost and capital commitment reduction, avoidance of major investments, improved ratios and others.

While this work is comprehensive, it is not intended to guide through the many phases of an outsourcing transaction, hence, it will not cover strategies of negotiations or performance measurement. It is not designed to meet the needs of the company that wants to know all the aspects of how to outsource some or all of its logistics functions.

This work will give an overview of selected issues that may arise during the outsourcing of a logistics function, putting the main emphasis on the planning stage as it is considered to be the critical factor in a successful outsourcing project. The most important decision during the outsourcing process is taken when the company is selecting its future partner[11]. This decision has a long-term affect on the company's everyday operations[12]. Hence, Chapter 5 covers the planning stage of an outsourcing project and discusses the vendor[13] selection process in detail.

It is important to note that, in this work, domestic is not distinguished from international outsourcing (also referred to as "offshoring"), it is rather concerned with outsourcing in general. As international considerations would involve numerous additional subjects as, for example, cultural issues or governmental regulations, it requires separate research demanding additional time and resources.

---

[11] cf. Changsen, Z. (2005). Third Party Logistics Management. Berlin: Logos Verlag. p. 22
[12] cf. ibid.
[13] There is not common usage of names for the organisation that outsources a function or for the organisation to which the function is transferred. Consequently, as common terminology throughout this work, the organisation that wishes to divest itself of a function is called the "company" or the "outsourcer", while the name of organisation that takes on these services is called the "vendor" or the "supplier" or "service provider".

1. Theoretical background

The perception of how to prevail in global competition has changed in the last decades[14]. During the 80s, top executives were concentrating on restructuring and delayering their corporations[15]. In the 90s the situation has changed. The decision making shifted to the ability to identify, cultivate, and exploit the core competencies of the company – to create the ongoing growth in the strongly competitive environment[16]. In the short run, a company's competitiveness is strongly dependent on the price/performance attributes of the product[17]. In the long run, however, competitiveness derives from the ability to create, at lower cost and less time than competitors, the core competencies that "spawn unanticipated products"[18].

1.1 The concept of core competence as a basis for outsourcing

Hamel and Prahalad discussed several risks of ignoring core competencies[19]. Among them are the weakened opportunities for growth, the dangerous dependence on outside suppliers of core products or the focus only on end products which leads to the lack of investment in development of new core competencies, to name just few[20]. Therefore, the core competence perspective should be a natural one in most companies. Some authors refer to Hamel and Prahalad in the context of their 1990 article, "The Core Competence of the Corporation", and attribute the concept to the rapid development of the outsourcing industry[21]. It has been noted that by understanding all the elements that enable the company to operate, managers can realise which ones are the

---

[14] cf. Goold, M. & Luchs, K. S. (1996). Managing the Multibusiness Company: strategic issues for diversified groups. London: Routledge. p. 218
[15] cf. ibid.
[16] cf. ibid.
[17] cf. ibid.
[18] ibid.
[19] cf. Hamel, G. & Prahalad, C. K. (1994). Competing for the Future. Boston: Harvard Business School Press. p. 221
[20] cf. ibid. pp. 221-222
[21] cf. Hamel, G. & Prahalad, C. K. (1990). The Core Competence of the Corporation. Boston: Harvard Business Review as cited by Benn, I. & Pearcy, J. (2002). Outsourcing: exploiting the skills of third parties. London: Hodder & Stoughton Educational. p. 5

sources of competitive advantage and which can by done by a third party[22]. Benn and Pearcy suggest that Michael Porter clarified this analysis by describing and explaining the concept of value chains[23] [24]. They argue that understanding of the value chain is of primary importance for the success of the outsourcing project, and if it is done correctly, the company understands each part of the chain beginning from the customer input to the service delivery, how they interrelate and which are core to competitive advantage[25]. If an organisation decides to outsource any of the elements its value chain to a third party, it will be successful as long as the client organisation retains responsibility for managing the connections between the elements and the strategic planning for each element, whether made or bought[26]. It would be important to note that Michael Porter also claims that an increase in production efficiency alone may not lead to the on-going competitive advantage[27]. The reason is that competitors can copy the achievements of companies and therefore reduce the uniqueness of its products, which leads to decrease in competitiveness[28]. Outsourcing certain function may become dangerous as the outsourced processes become less differentiated and do not demand special competencies for its fulfillment which increases the risk of imitation by competitors[29]. Therefore it is vital for success to identify processes employing core competencies, do not take them into outsourcing considerations and protect from reproducing by another party[30].

---

[22] cf. Hamel, G. & Prahalad, C. K. (1990). loc. cit.
[23] cf. Porter, M. (1985). Competitive Advantage: Creating and Sustaining Superior Performance. New York: The Free Press as cited by Benn, I. & Pearcy, J. loc. cit. p. 6
[24] The value chain categorizes the value-adding activities of an organisation. The "primary activities" include: inbound logistics, operations (production), outbound logistics, sales and marketing, and service (maintenance). The "support activities" include: administrative infrastructure management, human resources management, R&D, and procurement. The costs and value drivers are identified for each value activity. Source: Porter, M. ibid. p. 39
[25] cf. ibid.
[26] cf. ibid.
[27] cf. Porter, M. (1999). loc. cit.
[28] cf. ibid.
[29] cf. ibid.
[30] cf. ibid.

1.1.1 Identifying Core Competencies

To achieve long-term growth, companies need to develop, protect, and leverage their core competencies and consider outsourcing only those activities that do not confer a competitive advantage[31]. Identifying which resources and capabilities to preserve and which activities to outsource requires careful consideration and planning.

Prahalad and Hamel suggest three factors to help identify core competencies in any business:

- Access to a wide variety of markets: the key core competencies here are those that enable the creation of new products and services;
- A significant contribution to the perceived customer benefits: core competencies are the skills that enable a business to deliver a fundamental customer benefit, therefore it is essential for the company to identify those benefits;
- Difficulty for competitors to imitate: a core competence should be unique: in many industries, most skills can be considered a prerequisite for participation and do not provide any significant competitor differentiation. To qualify as core, a competence should be something that other competitors wish they had within their own business[32].

In the context of logistics authors offer additional key questions which are considered vital for identifying core competencies:

- Are there any special performance factors of the process which are not fulfilled by competitors[33]?
- Is the process exceptionally cost-efficient[34]?
- Is the quality of performance significantly higher than the one provided by

[31] cf. Müller-Dauppert, B. loc. cit. p. 12
[32] cf. Hamel, G. & Prahalad, C. K. (1994). loc. cit. pp. 224 *et. seq* ; cf. Müller-Dauppert, B. ibid.
[33] cf. Müller-Dauppert, B. ibid.
[34] cf. ibid.

competitors[35]?

- Is a need for future investments in the process that might be considered as core, not inevitable[36]?

If there are more positive answers than negative then the company should define the process as "core" and hense, accordingly protect and defend its properties in order to compete effectively in rapidly changing business world[37]. The statement that a systematic review of the existing processes is one of the first steps toward incorporating outsourcing in the business model is strongly supported in the modern business environment[38].

1.2 Outsourcing and supply chain management: common trends

Analysing some of the main trends that created the concept of supply chains one may recognize that primary drivers are comparable to those in outsourcing, which leads to the idea that outsourcing belongs to one of the main attributes of the modern supply chain management. The analysis shows that both concepts are strongly interrelated. The upper-discussed *concept of core competence*, *avoidance of high capital investments* and *short term focus* are some of the trends that stimulated the development of supply chains and the corresponding outsourcing decisions. C*ooperation management* is another key point in supply chain management and in outsourcing projects that establishes closer relationship between the two concepts.

1.2.1 Reduction of vertical integration and short term focus

The concept of core competence is also seen as a background for strategic planning in supply chain management[39]. Identifying the role of the company in

---

[35] cf. Müller-Dauppert, B. loc. cit.
[36] cf. ibid.
[37] cf. ibid.
[38] cf. McGill, D. (2004). Building a High Performance Business Model. Retrieved on-line in the Internet: http://www.accenture.com/Global/Services/By_Industry/Media_and_Entertainment/R_and_I/HighTools.htm. p. 2
[39] cf. Boutellier, R. & Corsten, D. (2000). Basiswissen Beschaffung. München: Carl Hanser Verlag as cited by Corsten, D. & Gabriel, C. (2004). Supply Chain Management erfolgreich umsetzen. Heidelberg: Physica-Verlag. pp. 19 *et. seq.*

the supply chain helps in the process of task sharing between suppliers[40]. The inevitable consequence is a distinctive reduction of vertical integration[41] which serves as another basis for outsourcing (please refer to Diagram 1)[42].

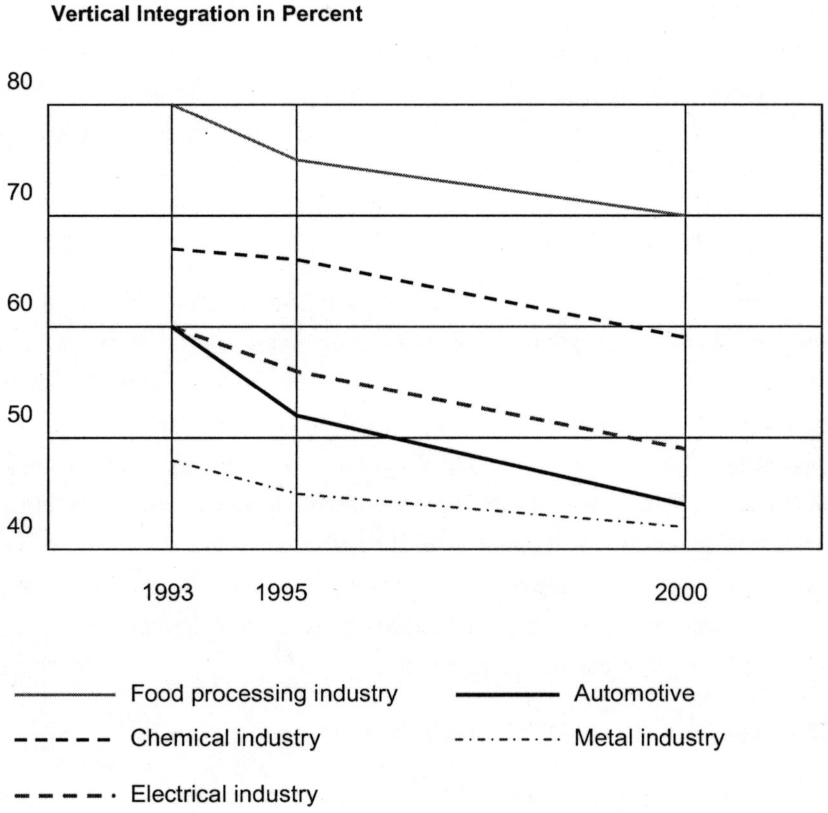

Diagram 1: Reduction of Vertical Integration as a consequence of core-competency focus

[40] cf. Boutellier, R. & Corsten, D. loc. cit.
[41] In microeconomics and strategic management, the term vertical integration describes a style of ownership and control. Vertically integrated companies are united through a hierarchy and share a common owner. Usually each member of the hierarchy produces a different product, and the products combine to satisfy a common need. Source: en.wikipedia.org/wiki/Vertical_integration
[42] cf. Boutellier, R. & Corsten, D. ibid.

Some authors are of the opinion that this trend found confirmation in practice: the importance of make-or-buy decision is growing as producers control smaller segments of supply chain[43]. Procurement is seen as a function which was mostly affected by this trend[44]. In the past, sourcing had a focus on raw materials and individual parts; nowadays the trend is shifting towards sourcing of the whole component assemblies[45].

In the effort to understand the success of the core-competency strategy in terms of its adoption by global companies, De Kok and Graves identify a number of circumstances that seem to characterize the late eighties business environment[46]. They claim that in the Western world the eighties were a time of relatively low economic growth and high unemployment rates which led to a *short-term focus*[47]. The core-competency strategy allowed companies to increase their return on investments (ROI) and related business performance indicators at the same time: outsourcing non-core competencies eliminated the associated fixed costs in the denominator of ROI, which positively affected the result[48]. The economic climate allowed multinational companies to outsource high-cost operations to companies with lower costs leading to immediate improvements in the balance sheets[49].

1.2.2 Avoidance of high capital investments

Another trend that links the concept of supply chains to outsourcing is avoiding high capital investments[50]. The improvements in labour productivity and process capabilities always required on-going investments[51]. By the end of the eighties, multinational companies with a tradition of capital-intensive manufacturing, such as electronics, white goods, automotive and consumer packaged goods (CPG),

---

[43] cf. Corsten, D. & Gabriel, C. loc. cit. p. 22
[44] cf. ibid. p. 23
[45] cf. ibid.
[46] cf. De Kok, A. G. & Graves S. C. (eds). (2003). Supply Chain Management: Design, Coordination and Operation. Amsterdam: ElsevierB.V. p. 2 *et. seq.*
[47] cf. ibid.
[48] cf. ibid.
[49] cf. ibid.
[50] cf. Bragg, S. M. (1998). Outsourcing. New York: John Wiley & Sons, Inc. pp. 2-3
[51] cf. ibid.

had invested for three decades in automation and mechanisation of manufacturing process[52]. The labour was replaced by capital, to the point that the capital-labour ratio approached that of primary industries, such as chemicals and metals[53]. Most of these vertically-integrated companies found that the added value was shifting upstream from assembly to fabrication and the need for investments in labour productivity and process improvements kept increasing[54]. Most companies decided to concentrate on their brands, implying that they concentrated on marketing and sales, and research and development of their products as well as on purchasing in order to increase their buying power[55]. This trend continues nowadays: in consumer packaged goods, for example, some manufacturers are pulling out of manufacture to concentrate on marketing and innovation[56]. Therefore upstream manufacturing activities were outsourced which continues to date[57].

1.2.3 SCM as core competence

Outsourcing activities allowed some companies to see their supply chain management as a core competence. Lee and Billington use Hewlett-Packard (HP) as an example of a company which recognized that SCM was one of its core competencies[58]. In parallel to concentration on research and development in software and printing technology, marketing and sales, and outsourcing manufacturing, HP successfully developed the skills for SCM. HP realised that one of its key success factors could be to offer both speed of delivery and product diversity to the market, and that this could be manageable without owing traditional manufacturing assets[59]. The product diversity was created as close as possible to the consumer, thereby for efficiencies upstream in SC[60].

---

[52] cf. De Kok, A. G. & Graves S. C. (eds). loc. cit. p. 3
[53] cf. ibid.
[54] cf. ibid.
[55] cf. ibid.
[56] cf. Lewis, C. (09/2003). Thinking outside the box in Logistics Europe Magazine. p. 29
[57] cf. De Kok, A. G. & Graves S. C. (eds). ibid.
[58] cf. Lee, H. L. & Billington, C. (1995). The Evolution of Supply Chain Management Models and Practice at Hewlett-Packard. Interfaces 25. pp. 42-63
[59] cf. ibid.
[60] cf. ibid.

Benn and Pearcy discuss Dell Computer Corporation as another example of a company that has made SCM its core competence[61]. Dell realises that to deliver effectively, it needs to understand its value chain in great detail[62]. Prior to Dell, personal computer (PC) manufacturers sold PCs through their dealer network, which required substantial capital investments in inventory by the dealers and increased risks for manufacturers[63]. In contrast, Dell decided to sell directly to the customer using the Internet as its marketing and sales channel[64]. Then it was possible to eliminate the final product inventory, as the company was able to assemble PCs for each customer order[65]. This example shows the potential for operating low-inventory, high-flexibility and customised-product supply chains. Outsourcing helps Dell to concentrate on sales while Welsh Western and Target are responsible for logistics function, and maintenance is handled through business partners Unisys and Getronics[66]. Today Dell is the number one supply chain company in the world (refer to the 2005 ranking presented in Appendices)[67].

1.2.4 Cooperation management

The interconnected links of material and information flows along the supply chain can only be achieved by managing relationships among partners[68]. Partnership is seen as one of the main principles of supply chain management and as well as of the outsourcing projects[69]. If supply chains want to be more than a pure addition of suppliers and customers, their management must have a lot in common with the management of strategic alliances[70]. Cooperation management in supply chains starts with the challenge of identifying the right

---

[61] cf. Benn, I. & Pearcy, J. loc. cit. p. 6
[62] cf. ibid.
[63] cf. ibid.
[64] cf. ibid.
[65] cf. ibid.
[66] cf. ibid. p. 7
[67] According to AMR Research Report "The Supply Chain Top 25" in Beschaffung Aktuell: Materialwirtschaft, Einkauf, Logistik (05/2005). p. 10
[68] cf. Seuring, S. (2003). loc. cit. p. 17
[69] cf. Corsten, D. & Gabriel, C. loc. cit. p. 213
[70] cf. Seuring, S. (2003). ibid.

partners within the value chain[71]. This process is just as important as a careful selection of the right vendor for outsourcing project following by the future cooperation between two parties. A key to building the new relationship is how both parties will monitor performance, evaluate the results, and solve the problems[72]. The relationship should be built on trust and shared commitment to success[73]. The only difference between SCM and outsourcing in this context would be that "...a supply chain is defined as a set of three or more entities (organisations or individuals)..."[74] Outsourcing project in turn usually deals with only two parties, which involves less complexity in communication process. An exception, however, would be the multi-vendor outsourcing (also referred to as multisourcing)[75]. Multisourcing requires a broader internal management equipped to manage cooperation with several vendors at a time which makes it similar to complexity of SCM[76].

Although the importance of cooperation is frequently mentioned in literature, only few instruments are described that help to face the challenges of supply chain management from the perspective of interpersonal cooperation[77]. Therefore this topic requires further research[78].

The issues discussed above shed some light on the development of supply chains and the role of outsourcing in this process. It should be clear that both concepts are interrelated and in many cases have similar objectives[79]. In order to get the clear picture of all SCM activities that can be outsourced, the correct definition of supply chain management is required.

---

[71] cf. Seuring, S. (2003). loc. cit. p. 225
[72] cf. Greaver, M. F. (1999). Strategic Outsourcing: A Structured Approach to Outsourcing Decisions and Initiatives. New York: AMACOM p. 29
[73] cf. ibid.
[74] Freiwald, S. (2005). Supply Chain Design. Frankfurt am Main: Peter Lang Verlag. p. 5
[75] cf. Mayer, A. G. & Söbbing, T. (2004). Outsourcing leicht gemacht. Frankfurt am Main: Redline Wirtschaft bei ueberreiter. p. 27
[76] cf. Halvey, J. K. & Melby, B. M. (2000). Business Process Outsourcing: Process, Strategies, and Contracts. New York: John Wiley & Sons, Inc. p. 32
[77] cf. Seuring, S. (2003). ibid. p. 226
[78] cf. ibid. p. 236
[79] The reduction of total costs is a frequently stated objective in supply chain management. It is also the most significant benefit of outsourcing as it will be shown in the following chapters.

2. Defining Supply Chain Management

Although the concept of Supply Chain Management is relatively young, its definition could serve as a separate topic for an empirical research, as there are already too many competing approaches to define the issue. Therefore only a selected range of relevant definitions will be discussed.

2.1 Definitions

Some authors (Freiwald, Seuring & Goldbach) refer to the definition of Handfield and Nichols:

> The supply chain encompasses all activities associated with the flow and transformation of goods from raw materials stage (extraction), through to the end user, as well as the associated information flows. Material and information flow both up and down the supply chain. Supply Chain Management is the integration of these activities through improved supply chain relationships, to achieve a sustainable competitive advantage.[80]

It is also evident (according to Freiwald[81], Schary/Skjott-Larsen[82], Seuring & Goldbach[83]), that the management of material and information flows links SCM to its conceptual basis in logistics[84]. While logistics aims at optimising material and information flows between single facilities, SCM looks much further, as the second part of the definition states[85].

---

[80] Handfield, R. B. & Nichols, E. L. loc. cit. p. 2 as cited by Seuring, S. & Goldbach, M. (eds). loc. cit. p. 17

[81] cf. Freiwald, S. loc. cit. pp. 9 *et. seq.*

[82] cf. Schary, P. B. & Skjott-Larsen, T. (1998). Managing the Global Supply Chain. Copenhagen: Copenhagen Business School Press. p. 17 *et. seq.*

[83] cf. Seuring, S. & Goldbach, M. (eds). ibid.

[84] cf. ibid.

[85] cf. ibid

Concerning the differences between SCM and logistics significant input is provided by the Council of Logistics Management (CLM). In 1998, the CLM modified its popular definition of logistics to a new one: "Logistics is a part of the supply chain process that plans, implements, and controls the efficient and effective flow and storage of goods, services, and related information from the point-of-origin to the point-of-consumption in order to meet customer's requirements"[86]. Although this definition of logistics stands for a very integrated approach, the CLM regards logistics as a subset of SCM. It is defined as: "Integrating and Managing Business Processes across the Supply Chain"[87]. Summarizing the attitude of the CLM two key messages can be derived:

- SCM is not a function, it is a holistic management concept
- SCM extends an integrated view of logistics. It integrates and manages key business processes across the supply chain.

Schönsleben's et. al. SCM definition focuses on the functions of the value chain and view of inter-organisational cooperation[88]. They describe SCM as the management of a strategic and long-term co-operation of logistical network members to develop, manufacture and distribute products[89]. Considering it from that perspective SCM can be defined as a special form of vertically integrating alliances[90].

Completing the list of the common views on SCM another aspect has to be mentioned: the development of information technology (IT)[91]. The role of IT has significantly gained importance in the 1990s[92]. The Internet as a worldwide available IT-infrastructure and the performance progress of IT architectures has

---

[86] Lambert, D. M. et. al. (1998). Supply Chain Management : Implementation Issues and Research Opportunities, in International Journal of Logistics Management, Vol. 9, No. 2, pp. 1-19 as cited by Changsen, Z. loc. cit. p. 5

[87] ibid.

[88] cf. Schönsleben, P. et. al. (2001). Nachhaltige Steigerung der Integration von Wertschöpfungsketten durch SCM. in Supply Chain Management, I/2001. pp. 15-25

[89] cf. ibid.

[90] cf. ibid.

[91] cf. De Kok, A. G. & Graves S. C. (eds). loc. cit. pp. 8-11

[92] cf. ibid.

created the basis for inter-organisational software applications (e.g. SAP APO to name the most popular system) enabling inter-company planning, execution and optimisation[93].

2.2 SCM perspectives with particular reference to outsourcing

Taking into account the upper-mentioned definitions, the following diagram has been outlined to represent the SCM perspectives and examples of corresponding outsourcing issues.

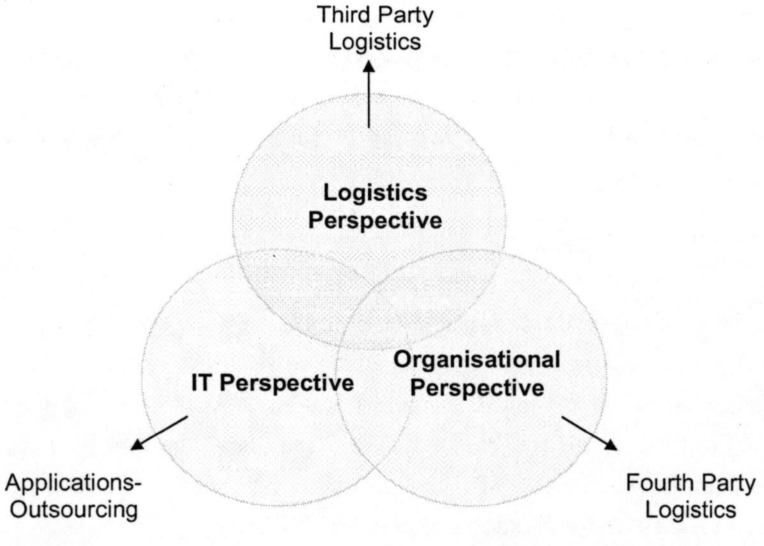

Diagram 2: The SCM perspectives and examples of corresponding outsourcing issues

In order to narrow the scope of this work, the examples of corresponding outsourcing issues will be discussed at a glance, providing its general understanding and relevance in the context of this work.

[93] cf. De Kok, A. G. & Graves S. C. (eds). loc. cit.

2.2.1 Applications outsourcing

Over the last two decades, IT outsourcing (or applications outsourcing[94]) has seen the largest volume of outsourcing in comparison to other functional areas in terms of the total cash volume of contracts signed[95]. As companies are structured to generate profitability from efficiency, there is a clear understanding of the importance of using the best technology[96]. The result is that IT outsourcers who are not able to invest heavily in getting the IT infrastructure tend to outsource it to external providers[97]. In the SCM context the quality if IT structures is vital for success. As noted above, the complexity of SC networks demands sophisticated systems for inter-organisational planning, execution and optimisation of processes. This is the reason why there has been given strong attention to the outsourcing of IT functions. Both the popular press and academic literature have recently covered IT outsourcing, thus this work will look at it superficially.

2.2.2 Forth Party Logistics

The Logistics Management Journal characterised Forth Party Logistics (4PL) as "the next generation for supply chain outsourcing"[98]. The concept belongs to one of the latest trends in SCM and shows enormous growth potential. According to the analysis by Frost & Sullivan Consulting, the total revenue in the European market for 4PL will increase from 4,7 billion Euro in 2002 to 13 billion Euro in 2010 (refer to Diagram 3 on page 22)[99].

Fourth Party Logistics providers offer analytic and decision-support capabilities, cutting-edge information technology, and competence in change management,

---

[94] cf. Hermes, H. J. & Schwarz, G. (eds). (2005). Outsourcing: Chansen und Risiken, Erfolgsfaktoren, rechtssichere Umsetzung. München: Haufe/Deloitte. p. 34

[95] cf. Bragg, S. M. (1998). Outsourcing. New York: John Wiley & Sons, Inc. p. 102

[96] cf. Benn, I. & Pearcy, J. loc. cit. p. 13

[97] cf. ibid.

[98] Foster, T. (1999). 4Pls: The next generation for supply chain outsourcing. Retrieved on-line in the Internet on the 21st of April 2006: http://www.logisticsmgmt.com/article/CA125187.html?text =fourth+party+logistics

[99] Frost & Sullivan Consulting. (2004). Junger Markt mit hohem Wachstumspotenzial in Marktbild Lager Magazine. p. 89

organisational development, and alliance management in addition to logistics management services[100]. In other words, they coordinate integration process of all participants along supply chains and implement inter-organisational planning, execution and control over logistical processes[101]. Therefore, the organisational perspective of SCM serves as a background for the importance of 4PL. Globalisation is another driving force in the development of 4PL[102]. The need for international cooperation with logistics service providers creates demand for organisational support and control over information flows, and execution of business processes[103]. As the concept is relatively young, there is a need for future academic research[104]. However, as the main emphasis of this work is placed on logistics perspective of SCM, the concept of 4PL will not be discussed in detail.

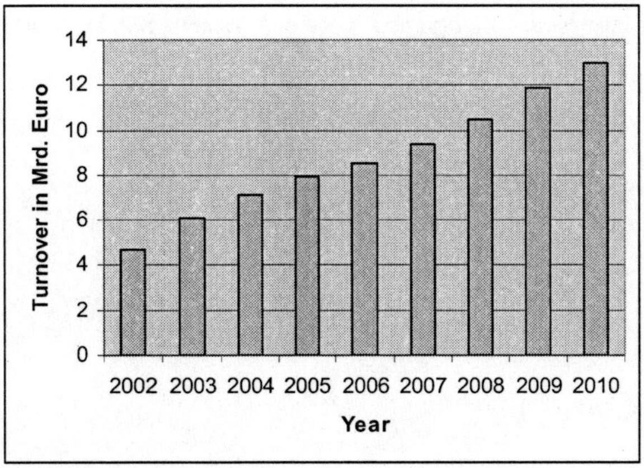

Diagram 3: European Market for Fourth Party Logistics

[100] cf. Copacino, W. (1998). A growing tidal wave of supply-chain outsourcing. Retrieved on-line in the Internet on the 24th of April 2006: http://www.logisticsmgmt.com/article/CA145525.html
[101] cf. Frost & Sullivan Consulting loc. cit.
[102] cf. ibid.
[103] cf. ibid.
[104] cf. Foster, T. loc. cit.

2.2.3 Third Party Logistics

The outsourcing of logistics services arouse when companies started to buy separate services from transportation companies (second party logistics or 2PL)[105]. That kind of outsourcing was normally based on simple make-or-buy decisions, choosing the cheapest alternative that meets service requirements[106]. Within the last years there has been a change in shipper-logistics provider arrangements[107]. While the primary driving forces previously were to reduce costs and release capital to alternative purposes, the driving forces today have a more strategic trust: to increase market coverage, improve the level of service or increase flexibility towards the changing requirements of customers[108]. Therefore outsourcing logistics services to 3PL providers became an important trend in supply chain management.

Hence, the aim of this work is to provide an insight into important issues concerning outsourcing of logistics services which will be implicated in the following chapters.

---

105 cf. Changsen, Z. loc. cit. p. 20
106 cf. ibid.
107 cf. ibid. p. 21
108 cf. ibid.

3. Logistics Outsourcing

Logistics has been an important part of every economy and every business entity. Logistics cost average about 12% of the World's GDP[109]. As discussed in previous chapters, avoidance of high capital investments, shorter product life cycles, incentives for cost savings and other factors have led many companies to outsource their logistics function to 3PL providers, so as to focus on their core competence.

3.1 Initial point

Logistics services is one of the areas where businesses have effectively found solutions with specialist providers and companies continue to see logistics as an area for potential saving although there are high set up costs[110]. Recent surveys show that in most cases if company profits are to fall, the transport and logistics budget would be the first to be cut[111]. Strategic and financial benefits make logistics outsourcing a growing business globally. Although outsourcing has grown across Europe as a whole, outsourcing as a trend differs from country to country (refer to diagram 4)[112].

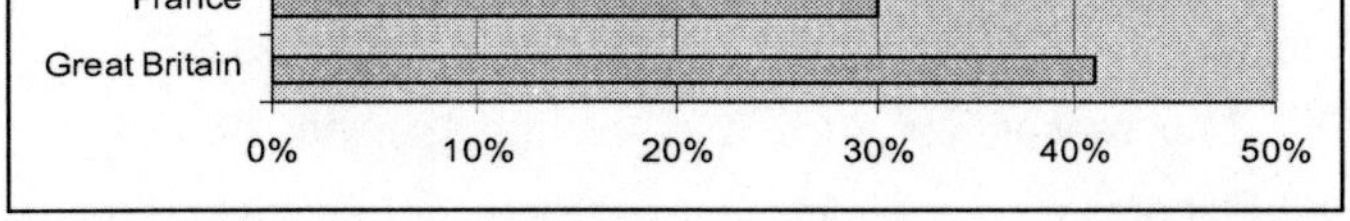

Diagram 4: Outsourcing volume in Europe as percentage of total logistics spending

---

[109] cf. Ballou, R. H. (1999). Business Logistics Management. Upper Saddle: Prentice Hall. p. 12
[110] cf. Lewis, C. loc. cit. p. 40
[111] cf. ibid.
[112] Dudek, F. & Weidt, S. (2004). Rahmendaten der Logistik. Fraunhofer IML / West LB

The UK is the most highly outsourced market with an estimated 41 per cent of the total logistics spending being outsourced in 2002[113]. The UK is also one of the largest markets in the EU in terms of total outsourced logistics spending in absolute figures[114]. This is in stark contrast to Germany – the largest market both in terms of total and outsourced spending – has a penetration of only 28 per cent[115]. However, the forecasts show that the volume of all outsourcing activities in Germany will increase in the future[116]. As shown in Diagram 5, the forecasted market volume of outsourcing-services in Germany will reach 16,2 billion Euro by the year 2008[117].

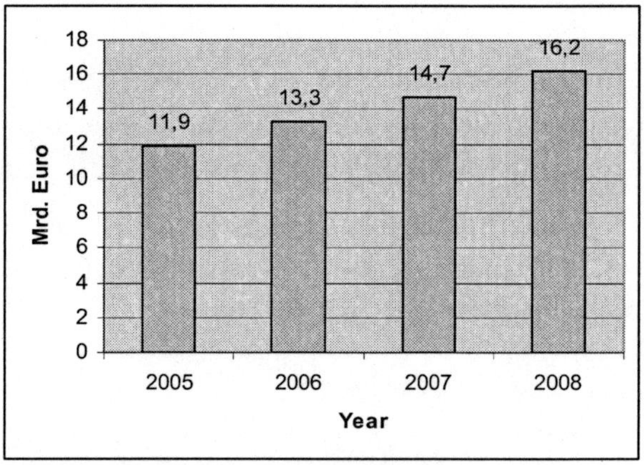

Diagram 5: Forecasted outsourcing volume in Germany

To summarize, third party logistics accounts for 10%-35% of the whole logistics market in Europe, a figure that is high compared to other countries[118]. Only in North America and Japan these figures are higher: at present, third party logistics providers handle 57% of logistics services in the USA and about 80% in Japan[119]. The reason for such a difference has not only an economical background, but also a cultural one. For example, in Italy, there has been a lack

[113] cf. Lewis, C. loc. cit.
[114] cf. ibid.
[115] cf. ibid.
[116] cf. Hermes, H. J. & Schwarz, G. loc. cit. p. 15
[117] cf. ibid.
[118] cf. Changsen, Z. loc. cit. p. 26
[119] cf. ibid.

of enthusiasm for externalising logistics operations as they are seen as an area of strategic advantage[120].

"The major logistics operators continue to position themselves effectively in the expected growth markets of Germany, Italy and Spain, where deeper penetration of outsourcing is anticipated."[121]

3.2 Logistics functions and its outsourcing potential

Classical transportation or warehousing, pre-assembly of vehicles in automotive industry, collection of unused drugs in pharmaceutical industry, or special after-sales-services in high-tech industry: the range of activities to outsource is becoming more and more versatile[122]. Therefore it is important to distinguish between different activities according to their outsourcing potential. Heptner, for example, divides logistics functions into three groups according to their relation to outsourcing: classical make-or-buy activities, advanced services and full service outsourcing[123]. Detailed list of all the activities is demonstrated in Diagram 6[124]:

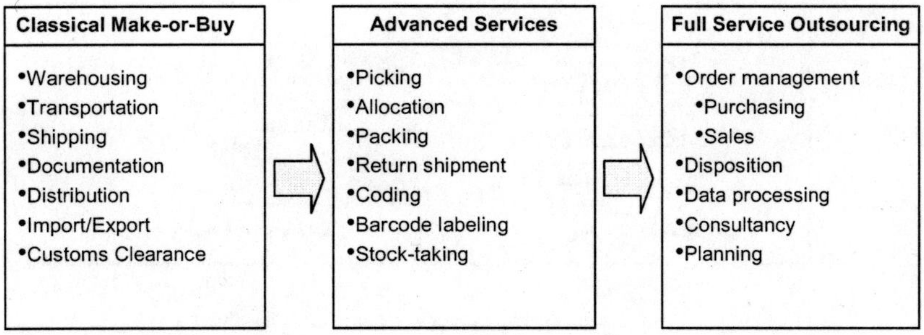

Diagram 6: Different kinds of logistics outsourcing activities

---

[120] cf. Lewis, C. loc. cit.
[121] ibid.
[122] cf. Scheja, K. & Jacob, P. (2005). Reibungslose Übergabe in Logistik Inside Magazine (10/2005). p. 37
[123] cf. Heptner, K. (1999). Praxisbeispiele und Bewertung von Dienstleistern in Workshop "Logistik-Dienstleistungen Richtig Einkaufen". Mülheim an der Ruhr: Europäisches Transportforum. p. 5
[124] cf. ibid.

Every activity can represent the certain level of competence in the company. If the competence is considered to be low, this automatically raises the issue of logistics attractiveness[125], which may lead to the possible outsourcing decision[126]. The decision should be positive if the improvements in own competence are too costly and/or complex, or if the process is not considered to be strategically important[127].

The classification of all processes according to its logistics attractiveness and strategic importance indicates the relevant outsourcing potential and serves as a basis for outsourcing considerations[128]. Müller-Dauppert demonstrated this approach with the help of the following diagram[129]:

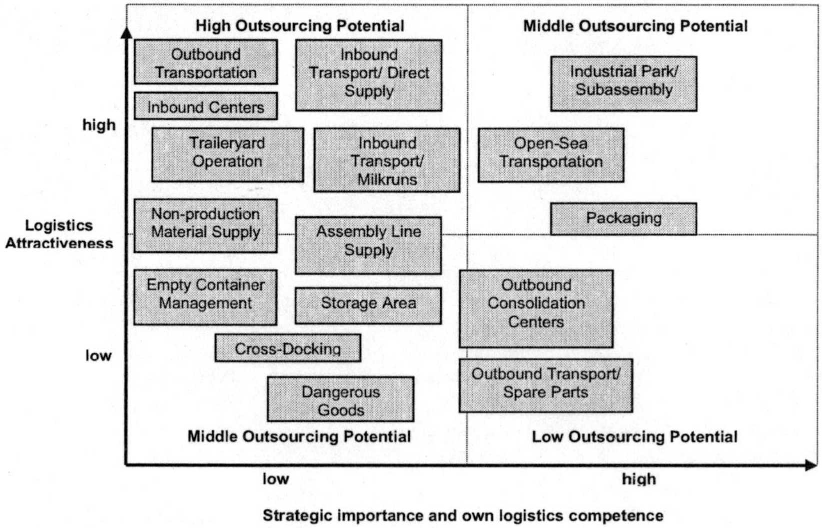

Diagram 7: Determination of outsourcing potential

[125] Under the term "logistics attractiveness" is meant the potential for cost savings or high efficiency. Source: cf. Müller-Dauppert, B. loc. cit. p. 12

[126] cf. Bund, M. & Bendixen, B. (1998). Outsourcing von Logistikleistungen in Unternehmensentwicklung und Industrial Engineering Magazine. Vol. 47. p. 125 as cited by Müller-Dauppert, B. ibid.

[127] cf. ibid.

[128] cf. ibid.

[129] cf. ibid.

To obtain a clear picture of the real-life situation that would be also reasonable to observe, what logistics functions are outsourced in practice. According to the 2005 survey by Cap Gemini, Georgia Institute of Technology, DHL and SAP, the following functions are considered to be the most popular in logistics outsourcing (refer to Diagram 8)[130].

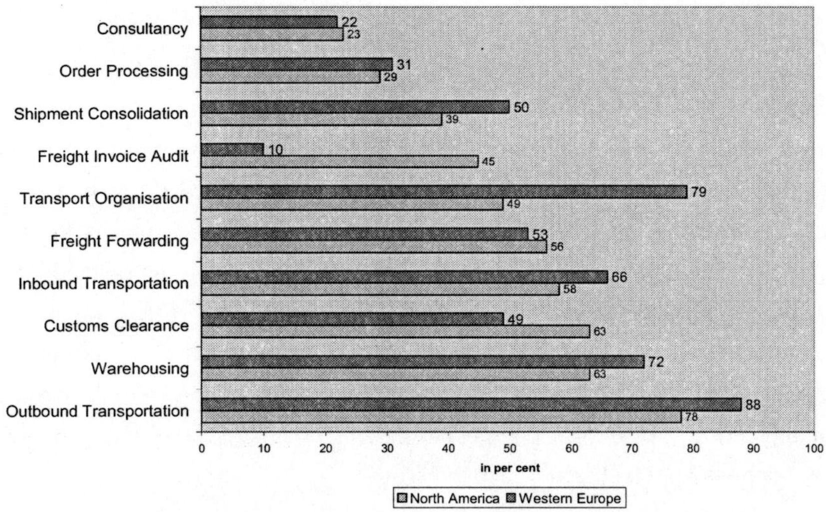

Diagram 8: Top 10 Outsourcing Functions

To concentrate on the most important (defined by the highest shares in outsourcing activities) logistics functions to outsource, they will be discussed in detail in the following part of the work. The USA logistics system will be taken as an example.

---

[130] The survey "Third Party Logistics 2005" was implemented by the consulting company Cap Gemini in cooperation with Georgia Institute of Technology, DHL and SAP. 1091 logistics and SC managers were asked. Among them 516 in North America, 339 in West Europe, 53 in Asia, 144 in Latin America, 31 in South Africa and 8 in the Middle East. The managers represent the following industries: vehicle construction, chemical, consumer goods, food and beverage, electronics, manufacturing, pharmaceutical industry, trade and telecommunications. Source: Kranke, A. (2005a). Preis schlägt Service in Logistik Inside Magazine. Vol. 12/2005. pp. 24-25

3.2.1 Transportation

Transportation provides logistical system geographical closure by linking facilities and markets[131]. In other words, transportation is the movement of goods and people between two points[132]. Transportation usually represents the most important single element in logistics costs for most firms[133]. Freight movement has been observed to absorb between one third and two thirds of total logistics costs[134].

It has been distinguished between inbound and outbound transportation[135], however different authors use different definitions of the same issue. Ballou and Coyle et.al., for example, distinguish between materials management and physical distribution[136]. Coyle et.al. claims that differences that may exist between materials management and physical distribution in terms of logistics requirements may have important implications for the design of a logistics system for the organisation[137]. The differences may be so great as to result in somewhat different designs of logistics systems for materials management and physical distribution[138]. Companies may find it convenient to view their logistics system from these two perspectives, and to have somewhat different management approaches for each may result[139].

---

131 cf. Bowersox, D. J. (1978). Logistical Management (2nd ed). New York: Macmillian Publishing Company. p. 111

132 cf. Murphy, P. R. & Woods, D. F. (2004). Contemporary Logistics (8th ed). Upper Saddle River: Pearson Education. p. 162

133 cf. Ballou, R. H. (2004). Business Logistics/Supply Chain Management. Upper Saddle River: Pearson Prentice Hall. p. 164

134 cf. ibid.

135 The terms "inbound" and "outbound" were introduced by Porter in the context of value chain activities, and referred to as inbound and outbound logistics. Under the term inbound logistics Porter defines activities associated with receiving, storing, and disseminating inputs to the product, such as material handling, warehousing, inventory control, vehicle scheduling and returns to suppliers. Outbound logistics includes activities associated with collecting, storing, and physically distributing the product to buyers, such as finished goods warehousing, material handling, delivery vehicle operation, order processing, and scheduling. Source: Porter, M. (1985). Competitive Advantage: Creating and Sustaining Superior Performance. New York: The Free Press p. 39

136 cf. Ballou, R. H. (1987). Basic Business Logistics. Englewood Cliffs: Prentice-Hall. pp. 23 *et. seq*; cf. Coyle, J. J. et. al. (1988). The management of Business Logistics, 4th ed. St. Paul, MN: West Publishing Company. p. 20

137 cf. Coyle, J. J. et. al. ibid.

138 cf. ibid.

139 cf. ibid.

Generally, a company has three alternative ways to obtain transportation capacity[140]. First, a private fleet of equipment may be purchased or leased; second, a company may engage the services of any legally authorized transport company that offers point-to-point transfer at specified charges[141]; or it can outsource its transportation needs to a transport specialist to provide movement service under the terms of specific contract[142]. Last alternative is also referred to as contract carriage, third-party logistics or integrated logistics[143]. According to numerous surveys, and as it has been shown above, transportation is the most popular function to outsource.

3.2.2 Warehousing

Warehousing is generally defined as the storage of goods before their use[144]. A more detailed definition is provided by Murphy & Woods who refer to the concept as "that part of a firm's logistics system that stores products at and between points of origin and point of consumption."[145] In broader sense, this definition includes a wide spectrum of facilities and locations that provide warehousing, including the storage of iron ore in open fields, the storage of finished goods in the production facility, and the storage of raw materials, industrial goods, as well as finished goods while they are in transport[146]. It also includes highly specialized storage facilities such as bean and grain elevators, tobacco warehouses, potato cellars, and refrigeration facilities[147].

A growing trend in today's warehousing environment is the use of the third party warehousing concept (also referred to as contract warehousing)[148]. Contract warehousing thus provides another example of logistics outsourcing. Its popularity is growing substantially that reflects a general acceptance of the

---

[140] cf. Bowersox, D. J. et. al. (1986). Logistical Management (3rd ed). New York: Macmillian Publishing Company. p. 23

[141] Also referred to as Common Carriage

[142] cf. Bowersox, D. J. et. al. ibid.

[143] cf. ibid; cf. Ballou, R. H. (2004). loc. cit. pp. 720-722

[144] cf. Taff, C. (1972). Management of Physical Distribution and Transportation, 5th ed. Homewood: Irwin. p. 172

[145] Murphy, P. R. & Woods, D. F. loc. cit. p. 299

[146] cf. Coyle, J. J. et. al. loc. cit. p. 248

[147] cf. ibid.

[148] cf. Murphy, P. R. & Woods, D. F. ibid.

outsourcing philosophy by many organisations; moreover, warehousing is one of the most frequently outsourced logistics activities[149]. The third party warehousing company specializes in providing efficient, economical and accurate distribution services[150]. These services include not only basic storage but also a package of logistics support services that range from handling and managing inventory to processing and shipping customer orders[151]. Being a part of a partnership, the warehousing firm provides services, for example, for manufacturer so that it can concentrate on its core functions such as producing and marketing the product[152]. The 3P warehousing company makes available the following customized logistics services: storage, break-bulk, consolidation, order management, spot stocking, in-transit mixing, inventory control, transportation arrangement and other additional logistics support services[153].

3.2.3 Shipment consolidation

A significant opportunity exists in all logistical operations to reduce transportation expenditures through shipment consolidation[154]. The nature of transportation costs is that it costs less on a per-unit-of-weight basis to ship a larger quantity[155]. This is because certain costs (fixed, administrative, or terminal) are the same per shipment: hence, when the shipment is larger, such costs can be allocated over a larger weight[156]. The transportation manager is therefore often trying to consolidate large numbers of small shipments into small number of large shipments[157]. To reduce transportation cost a great deal of attention has been directed to the development of consolidation programs[158]. From the operational point of view, three opportunities exist to realize freight

[149] cf. Murphy, P. R. & Woods, D. F. loc. cit. p. 299
[150] cf. Coyle, J. J. et. al. loc. cit.
[151] cf. ibid.
[152] cf. ibid.
[153] cf. Bowersox, D. J. (1986). Third Party Partner – a timely concept. Columbus, Ohio: Ackerman as cited by cf. Coyle, J. J. et. al. ibid. p. 275
[154] cf. Murphy, P. R. & Woods, D. F. loc. cit. pp. 226-231; cf. Ballou, R. H. (1987). loc. cit. p. 348; cf. Ballou, R. H. (2004). loc. cit. pp. 252-254
[155] cf. Murphy, P. R. & Woods, D. F. ibid.
[156] cf. ibid.
[157] cf. ibid.
[158] cf. ibid.

consolidation: market area grouping, schedule delivery and pool consolidation[159].

Market area grouping is the most fundamental type of consolidation when small shipments to a specific market area are combined for transportation[160]. This type of consolidation does not interrupt with natural flow of the freight by trying to influence when shipment are tendered to common carrier[161]. Rather the quantity being shipped to or purchased by customers in the overall market provide the consolidation basis[162]. Many firms participate in purchasing cooperatives that arrange multi-shipper consolidations[163].

Scheduled distribution consists of limiting shipments to specific markets to selected days each week[164]. The scheduled distribution plan is normally communicated to customers in a way that sells the virtue of planned delivery[165]. The performance cycle is stabilized by a commitment on the part of the shipping firm that orders received prior to an established deadline will be guaranteed to be delivered on the day of scheduled distribution[166].

Pool consolidation represents another example of outsourcing[167]. Participation in a pooled distribution plan typically means that a third-party organisation arranges the consolidation[168]. That may be a freight forwarder or a public warehouse that consolidates shipments from different organisations[169].

3.2.4 Freight Forwarding

Freight forwarding is analysed by some authors (Murphy, P. R. & Woods; Coyle, J. J. et. al.) as another consolidation alternative[170]. The two types of domestic freight forwarders – surface and air – can be best thought of as

---

[159] cf. Bowersox, D. J. et. al. loc. cit. pp. 58-60
[160] cf. ibid.
[161] cf. ibid.
[162] cf. ibid.
[163] cf. ibid.
[164] cf. Coyle, J. J. et. al. loc. cit. p. 399
[165] cf. ibid.
[166] cf. ibid.
[167] cf. Bowersox, D. J. et. al. ibid.
[168] cf. ibid.
[169] cf. ibid.
[170] cf. Murphy, P. R. & Woods, D. F. loc. cit. pp. 168-169; cf. Coyle, J. J. et. al. ibid.

consolidators of freight[171]. The domestic surface freight forwarder collects small shipments from shippers, consolidates these shipments into large loads, and presents to railroads or motor carriers for the intercity movement[172]. At destination, the freight forwarder breaks the load down into individual shipments and delivers them to the correct consignee[173]. The freight forwarder realizes its revenue from the difference between the high less-than-volume rate paid by the shipper, and the lower volume rate assessed by the carrier the freight forwarder uses[174]. The main advantage of outsourcing small shipments to freight forwarder is lower transit time[175].

A company that has little expertise with international shipping should consider outsourcing its international transportation needs to foreign freight forwarder[176]. The foreign freight forwarder employs individuals that are knowledgeable in all aspects of international shipping[177]. Like their domestic counterparts, foreign freight forwarders consolidate small shipments into more economical sizes which in the international arena range from containers up to entire ships[178]. They also take care of the routine actions required for international shipments, including the following functions:

- Preparing commercial invoices
- Obtaining export licenses
- Issuing export declarations for the shipper
- Obtaining and preparing consular invoices
- Paying freight charges
- Presenting documents to the bank or forwarding them to other destinations
- Chartering vessels or obtaining necessary space
- Obtaining dock receipts

---

171 cf. Murphy, P. R. & Woods, D. F. loc. cit.
172 cf. Coyle, J. J. et. al. Loc. cit.
173 cf. ibid.
174 cf. Murphy, P. R. & Woods, D. F. ibid.
175 cf. ibid.
176 cf. Coyle, J. J. et. al. ibid.
177 cf. ibid.
178 cf. ibid.

- Obtaining port warehousing space and more[179].

Since no two international sales are exactly alike and since shippers have different capabilities for international traffic, the forwarder usually perform certain part of the export work[180]. The logistics manager must compare the forwarder's cost to the cost hiring additional personnel to find out whether outsourcing decision is economically right.

3.2.5 Invoice audit

Human mistakes commonly cause the extra expense of performing audits. In the control of transportation costs, many firms have found it worthwhile to audit their freight bills[181]. Errors in rates, product descriptions, weights and routing are just a few of the ways that errors can creep into billing. It is common for a large company to have up to 750,000 invoices a year, and even infrequent errors can result in sizable overcharges[182]. There is a 3 to 5 per cent overcharge to freight bills on an annual basis[183].

Checking bills can be handled by a company's traffic department; however, many firms prefer to have this audit performed outside the firm by freight bill auditing companies[184]. These firms offer this service on a commission basis. That is, the audit firm receives a percentage of the claims that are recovered[185]. Outsourcing auditing to an outside agency is particularly beneficial to the small companies that can not efficiently provide a staff for this activity[186].

---

179 cf. Brooks, D. L. (1972). Exporting without tears in Transportation and Distribution Management Magazine (12/1972). p. 44 as cited by Coyle, J. J. et. al. loc. cit.
180 cf. ibid.
181 cf. Ballou, R. H. (2004). loc. cit. p. 740
182 cf. ibid.
183 cf. ibid.
184 cf. Ballou, R. H. (1987). loc. cit. p. 177
185 cf. ibid.
186 cf. ibid.

4. Benefits and potential pitfalls of outsourcing

In order to discuss the degree to which logistics operations are successfully outsourced and to find out what the related risks are, a detailed discussion on the most significant benefits and potential pitfalls is given in the following part of the work.

4.1 Benefits of outsourcing

After the outsourcing potential of a function is identified as high, arises the question, what chances may bring the outsourcing decision, and if this decision is in line with the strategic objectives of the company[187]. Another important question is whether outsourcing is influencing company's efficiency in a positive way. In order to answer these questions one may refer to Schweiger[188], Bragg[189], Benn & Pearcy[190], Müller-Dauppert[191], Köhler-Frost[192], Hermes & Schwarz[193] and Horngren[194] to analyse the following benefits of outsourcing:

- Cost reduction
- Concentration on core competencies[195]
- Avoidance of major investments
- Wider skills pool
- Quality of service
- Higher flexibility
- Improved ratios
- Transformation of fixed costs into variable costs
- Reduction of capital commitment

---

[187] cf. Müller-Dauppert, B. loc. cit. p. 14

[188] cf. Schweiger, S. (2005). Gefahr droht immer in Beschaffung Aktuell Magazine April 2005. p. 34 *et. seq.*

[189] cf. Bragg, S. M. loc. cit. pp. 3 *et. seq.*

[190] cf. Benn, I. & Pearcy, J. loc. cit. pp. 8 *et. seq.*

[191] cf. Müller-Dauppert, B. ibid.

[192] cf. Köhler-Frost, W. (ed). (2005). Outsourcing: Schlüsselfaktoren der Kundenzufriedenheit. Berlin: Schmidt Verlag. pp. 38 *et. seq.*

[193] cf. Hermes, H. J. & Schwarz, G. loc. cit. pp. 15 *et. seq.*

[194] cf. Horngren, C. T. et. al. loc. cit. p. 58

[195] For the detailed discussion on the concept of core competence refer to Chapter 1

The main benefits of outsourcing from the managers' point of view are listed in the Diagram 9[196]:

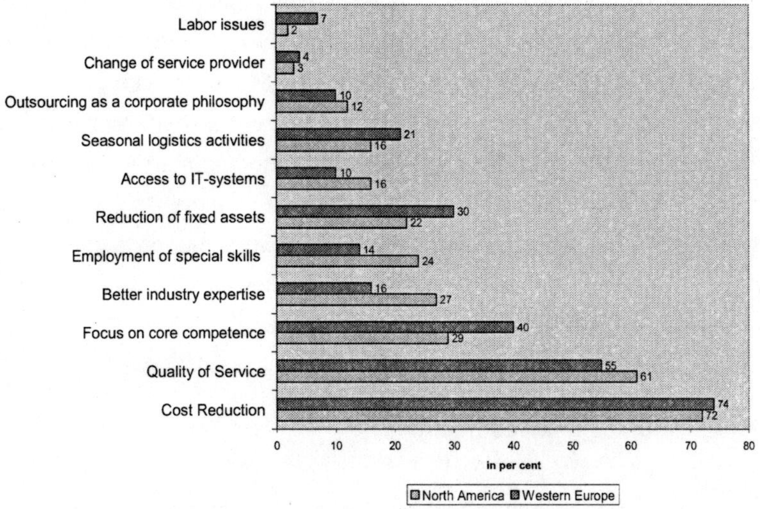

Diagram 9: Benefits of Outsourcing from managers' point of view

4.1.1 Cost reduction

The number one priority for companies is to reduce costs, as indicated in numerous surveys and empirical researches (also refer to the Diagram 9). In four out of five outsourcing projects cost reduction was on the top of the agenda[197]. A company may emphasize cost savings for a variety of reasons, such as being in a poor financial position, or because of a goal to increase profits[198]. There are some situations in which a company can reduce its costs by outsourcing. For example, a supplier has clearly lower costs if it can

[196] Kranke, A. (2005a). loc. cit.
[197] cf. Weber, J. & Engelbrecht, C. (2002). In fremden Händen in Logistik Heute Magazine, 9/2002. pp. 38-39
[198] cf. Bragg, S. M. loc. cit. pp. 4 *et. seq.*

centralize the work of several companies at one location, such as a central truck maintenance facility[199].

But the most significant cost savings in logistics outsourcing are caused by the differences in compensation of operative personnel[200]. For example the collective agreement in logistics (ver.di[201]) includes 13% longer labour time and 30% less salary in comparison with the collective agreement of IG Metall[202] [203]. Another example of cost savings is the difference in internal regulations between industrial companies and logistics service providers[204]. The rules for accident prevention and fire protection requirements, for instance, allow fivefold stacking of pallet cages, which in turn is not allowed in some industrial companies where only threefold stacking is permitted[205]. This leads to higher storage costs and serves as a reason for outsourcing considerations[206].

4.1.2 Avoidance of major investments[207]

A company may find that it has a function that is not as efficient as it could be, due to a lack of investment in it, which may demand additional investments in order to modernize it[208]. By outsourcing the function, the company can permanently avoid this investment. For example, a company that owns an old transportation fleet can sell the fleet to a supplier, who will provide an upgraded fleet to the company as part of its service[209].

---

[199] cf. Bragg, S. M. loc. cit.
[200] cf. Kranke, A. (2005b). Da muss jeder durch in Logistik Inside Magazine. Vol. 10/2005. p. 44
[201] ver.di is a large German trade union. It claims to be the largest trade union in the world, with 2.6 million members. "ver.di" is an abbreviation for Vereinte Dienstleistungsgewerkschaft, which stands for "united trade union for the services sector" and includes logistics services. Source: en.wikipedia. org/wiki/Ver.di
[202] IG Metall (Industriegewerkschaft Metall - German Metalworkers' Union) is the dominant metalworkers' union in Germany. Analysts of German labour relations consider it a major trend-setter in national bargaining. As a metalworkers' union, it represents the labour of the auto industry. Source: en.wikipedia.org/wiki/IG_Metall
[203] cf. Kranke, A. (2005b). ibid.
[204] cf. Müller-Dauppert, B. loc. cit. p. 15
[205] cf. ibid.
[206] cf. ibid.
[207] The discussion on avoidance of major investments is also presented in this work in Chapter 1
[208] cf. Bragg, S. M. ibid. pp. 2 *et. seq*
[209] cf. ibid.

4.1.3 Wider skills pool

A company may find that its in-house skill set is inadequate for a given function, which may result in minimal improvements to the function in the future, if any[210]. A company can overcome this problem by handing over the function to the supplier, who specializes in that function and who therefore is highly competent in its administration, using well-trained and experienced staff as well as the most current procedures and technological advances[211]. This reason is most commonly used for outsourcing those functions that require high skills levels, such as supply chain planning and optimisation, which usually is outsourced to consulting agencies.

4.1.4 Quality of service

Delivery reliability and completeness, timing, and other quality factors sometimes are performed better by another party[212]. The key to success in logistics is the required process know-how, well educated and experienced staff members and a modern IT system[213]. In practice not every logistics service provider tends to invest heavily in technical solutions, but even the simple warehouse management system[214] (WMS) or item scanner, or Pick-by-Voice[215] system allow reaching the high level of quality[216]. In addition, some companies provide their employees with rewards according to their job performance and quality of service[217].

---

[210] cf. Bragg, S. M. loc. cit. p. 2
[211] cf. ibid.
[212] cf. ibid.
[213] cf. ibid. p. 17
[214] Warehouse Management System is a key part of the supply chain and provides directed stock rotation, intelligent picking directives, automatic consolidation and cross-docking to maximize the use of valuable warehouse space. The systems also direct and optimises stock put-away based on real-time information about the status of bin utilization. Source: en.wikipedia.org/wiki/Warehouse_Management_System
[215] Pick-by-Voice system enables a voucherless communication with the warehouse management system and minimizes the administrative effort of the picking process. The result is a steady going work flow without interruptions such as editing picking lists, scanning barcodes or lengthy data typing. Source: http://www.logim-software.com/englisch/produkte/pdf/pickbyvoice_factssheet.pdf
[216] cf. Müller-Dauppert, B. loc. cit.
[217] cf. ibid.

4.1.5 Higher flexibility

Following the "make" strategy means investment in logistics infrastructure, which totals in the case of trading corporations double or triple-digit million euro volumes[218]. By the in the retail industry typical 1-2% return-on-sales (ROS), that kind of investment should be planned at least 10 years in advance, which may even require up to 12-15 years as the planning is usually based on past knowledge[219]. In logistics that kind of time horizon is too long and short-term changes in strategy lead to acceptance of sunk costs[220] [221]. Therefore, outsourcing of logistics functions significantly raises the flexibility of strategic decision making as the additional resources are acquirable through another logistics service provider[222]. Additionally, any potential change in demand or strategy is to be regarded in the outsourcing contract (whether limited in time or prolongable), so that in case of new requirements the issue would be legally allowed[223].

4.1.6 Improved ratios

Some companies are so driven by their performance ratios that they will outsource functions solely to improve them[224]. For example, outsourcing a function that involves transferring assets to the supplier will increase the company's return on assets (which is one of the most important measurements for many companies)[225]. The functions most likely to improve this ration are those heavy in assets, such as transportation or warehousing. Another ratio that

---

[218] cf. Pfohl, H. C. (ed). (2004). Erfolgsfaktor Kooperation in der Logistik. Berlin: Erich Smidt Verlag. p. 84

[219] cf. ibid.

[220] In economics and in business decision-making, sunk costs are costs that have already been incurred and which cannot be recovered to any significant degree. Because sunk costs have been irrevocably expended or committed, they are not considered in the cost/benefit analysis. Source: www.acf.hhs.gov/programs/cb/dis/sacwis/cbaguide/appendixb.htm

[221] cf. Pfohl, H. C. (ed). ibid.

[222] cf. ibid.

[223] cf. ibid.

[224] cf. Bragg, S. M. loc. cit. p. 3

[225] cf. ibid.

can be improved is profitability per person[226]. To enhance this, a company should outsource all functions involving large number of employees.

4.1.7 Transformation of fixed costs into variable costs

In addition to weighing the varied effects of changes in fixed and variable costs, managers need to consider their firm's ratio of fixed to variable costs, called *operating leverage*[227]. In highly leveraged companies – those with high fixed costs and low variable costs – small changes in sales volume result in large changes in net income[228]. Accordingly, companies with less leverage are not affected as much by changes in sales which make them more flexible. Sharp decreases in demand or poor planning abilities lead to inefficient allocation of resources and personnel which can be improved by outsourcing[229].

4.1.8 Reduction of capital commitment

The typical dilemma of many companies is whether to invest in logistic facilities or better in other business activities. On one side, there is a pressure from shareholders to optimise debt/equity ratio[230], to achieve required return on capital and appropriate return on assets, to increase sales per employee etc. aiming at increasing the shareholder value[231]. And on the other side there are external challenges such as Basel II[232] where the ranking of the company and by that its cost of capital are dependent on the risks the company is exposed to[233]. This framework leads to the careful examination of every investment decision. Every investment option is thoroughly analysed with respect to its

[226] cf. Bragg, S. M. loc. cit. p. 3
[227] cf. Horngren, C. T. et. al. loc. cit. p. 58
[228] cf. ibid.
[229] cf. Müller-Dauppert, B. loc. cit. p. 15
[230] Debt/Equity Ratio – indicator of financial leverage. The higher the level of debt, the greater the fixed costs, and thus the more operational risk assumed. Source: www.powerinvestor.com/
[231] cf. Müller-Dauppert, B. ibid. p. 16
[232] Basel II is a round of deliberations by central bankers from around the world, under auspices of the Basel Committee on Banking Supervision in Basel, Switzerland, aimed at producing uniformity in the way banks and banking regulators approach risk management across national borders. Source: www.bis.org/publ/bcbsca.htm
[233] cf. Müller-Dauppert, B. ibid.

necessity and make-or-buy decision (concerning single objects such as leasing of machinery or processes - e.g. sourcing of logistic services)[234]. The same concerns are taken into account while deciding on disinvestment[235]. Cash resources may be used for investments in other business processes or simply increases the shareholder attractiveness and credibility[236].

The above-mentioned points are referred to as the most significant benefits of outsourcing. Other advantages to name would include synergy effects[237], utilisation of special competences[238] and potential increase in customer satisfaction[239]. However, the process of outsourcing is also associated with numerous risks which need to be taken into consideration.

4.2 Potential pitfalls of outsourcing

While there are many good reasons to outsource a function, there is also a number of risks related to this decision. These can range from minor pricing issues to non-performance by a supplier of the outsourced function[240]. The company making the outsourcing decision must be aware of these risks before making the decision to hand over a function to a vendor[241]. According to recent literature the major perils of outsourcing in logistics are:

- Poor or non-performance[242]
- Loss of logistics know-how[243]
- Start up difficulties[244]

---

[234] cf. Müller-Dauppert, B. loc. cit. p. 16
[235] cf. ibid.
[236] cf. ibid.
[237] cf. Pfohl, H. C. (ed). ibid. p. 83
[238] cf. Bragg, S. M. loc. cit. p. 3
[239] cf. Köhler-Frost, W. (ed). loc. cit. p. 38
[240] cf. Bragg, S. M. loc. cit. p. 7
[241] cf. ibid.
[242] cf. ibid.
[243] cf. Engelbrecht, C. (2004). Logistikoptimierung durch Outsourcing. Wiesbaden: Deutscher Universitäts-Verlag. p. 22
[244] cf. Müller-Dauppert, B. loc. cit. p. 18

- Loss of motivation[245]
- Business transition and social plan[246]
- Dependency on the vendor[247]

What the perceived failure factors are in practice is demonstrated by the Outsourcing Logistics Survey 2006 results[248]. However, it should be noted that while companies are quick to announce their success stories, they are understandably somewhat reluctant to report their failures[249].

The most likely factors that can make one's outsourcing strategy fail are illustrated in Diagram 10[250]:

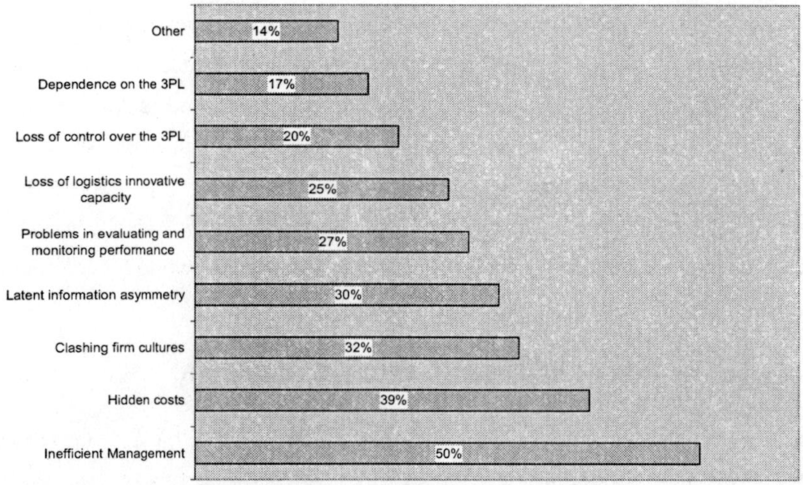

Diagram 10: Failure factors in logistics outsourcing

[245] cf. Pfohl, H. C. (ed). loc. cit. p. 85
[246] cf. Bragg, S. M. loc. cit. and cf. Müller-Dauppert, B. loc. cit.
[247] cf. Engelbrecht, C. loc. cit.
[248] *Eyefortransport* conducted the "Outsourcing Logistics 2006 – Europe Fortune 500 shippers' views on their 3PL partnerships" Report during September and October 2005. The survey drew responses from 312 Fortune 500 logistics professionals. Source: http://www.eyefortransport.com/outsourceuro/report.shtml
[249] cf. *Eyefortransport*. (2006). Outsourcing Logistics 2006 Report. Retrieved on-line in the Internet on the 17th of May 2006. p. 10
[250] cf. ibid.

Some of the most common risks presented in recent literature will now be discussed in detail.

4.2.1 Poor or non-performance

In some cases the vendor's situation may change in the future, causing problems in the outsourcing relationship[251]. For example, the vendor may have financial difficulties, be acquired by another company that has different approach to outsourcing, or undergo a shift in strategy that forces it to provide different services[252]. These risks can be lowered by ensuring that all the outsourcing services and related activities are listed in the contract and, in addition, there is a termination clause that allows the company to back out of the contract if any of the above-mentioned circumstances take place[253]. The quality of an outsourcing contract serves as a basis for the success of the whole project[254]. Moreover, special attention should be paid to the request for proposal that demands careful and detailed description of all the activities associated with the outsourcing process[255]. If all the procedures are implemented professionally, then the risk of poor or non-performance is minimised, however, it can not be completely eliminated as the business world is changing dynamically influencing organisational and stuff structures[256].

4.2.2 Loss of logistics know-how

Another possible consequence of outsourcing is the loss of logistics know-how[257]. This risk becomes imminent in the case if the company decides to reintegrate the outsourced function and to execute it internally[258]. The damage can, however, be acceptable if the function cannot be described as strategically

---

[251] cf. Bragg, S. M. loc. cit. p. 7
[252] cf. Bragg, S. M. ibid.
[253] cf. Hermes, H. J. & Schwarz, G. loc. cit. p. 24; cf. Bragg, S. M. ibid.
[254] cf. Hermes, H. J. & Schwarz, G. ibid.
[255] cf. Müller-Dauppert, B. loc. cit. p. 21
[256] cf. ibid.
[257] cf. Engelbrecht, C. loc. cit. p. 22 and cf. Pfohl, H. C. (ed). loc. cit. p. 84 as well as cf. Hermes, H. J. & Schwarz, G. ibid. p. 23
[258] cf. ibid.

important and doesn't belong to the core competences directly influencing a successful operation[259]. Pfohl argues, in turn, that the loss of know-how can be eliminated in the case of close collaboration between partners[260]. And partnership with different logistics service providers may even provide a basis for future improvements in the own logistics know-how[261]. Crucial factors here are: the exercise of the management function, controlling of the performance and the on-going benchmarking aimed at defining the optimal processes both for service provider and the bidder[262]. Knowledge about the possible implications of the actions that influence the logistics performance is therefore an imperative basis for cooperation[263].

4.2.3 Start up difficulties

The most common start up difficulties may include following factors: IT problems (especially if the record data should be processed manually), or processes are not completely realised by the service provider (in case of high complexity), or time limits set are too ambitious (highly qualified vendors are characterised by realistic estimations and adequate reporting system), or the resources are not sufficient[264]. Those factors are sometimes underestimated during planning, therefore it is advisable for both parties to employ experienced project managers or to appoint a consulter who will support the project on the early stages of implementation[265].

4.2.4 Loss of motivation

Restructuring and redundancy arrangements in the company always involve decrease in the level of employee motivation[266]. Departments influenced by outsourcing (whether by release of employees or transfer to other company)

---

[259] cf. Hermes, H. J. & Schwarz, G. loc. cit. p. 23
[260] cf. Pfohl, H. C. (ed). loc. cit. pp. 84-85
[261] cf. ibid.
[262] cf. ibid.
[263] cf. ibid.
[264] cf. Müller-Dauppert, B. loc. cit. p. 21
[265] cf. ibid.
[266] cf. Pfohl, H. C. (ed). ibid. p. 85

may face the decrease in performance of up to 20-30%[267]. In addition to inferior performance, there is also an external impact on the customers, shareholders and suppliers, who are likely to be affected by the frustrated spirit of unsatisfied employees[268]. An intensive and consistent communication aimed at explaining the reasons, progress and future proceeding of the outsourcing project can help to abolish the fear and misunderstanding among employees[269].

4.2.5 Business transition and social plan

A very serious risk, especially for a large company that dominates a local economy, is that there can be significant fallout within the community if the company lays off a large number of workers as a result of an outsourcing arrangement[270]. There are numerous outsourcing deals where employees are not rehired by the vendor, which can generate a significant effect, especially if the local area is highly dependent on the company to maintain the local economy[271]. One way to mitigate this risk is to choose only those vendors who guarantee that they will hire a large proportion of the company's employees and retain them for a certain period of time (such as a minimum of one year)[272].
In Germany this problem was reflected in the Civil Code[273]. § 613a serves as a protective function, stipulating that in case of transfer real property, operating facilities and employees must be accepted by other party (full text of the article is presented in Appendices)[274]. This includes also protection against dismissal (at least one year), pension arrangements and special rules for compensation[275]. This forces the vendor to accept more employees then needed including workers with insufficient level of qualification and motivation.

---

[267] cf. Pfohl, H. C. (ed). loc. cit.
[268] cf. Müller-Dauppert, B. loc. cit. p. 22
[269] cf. ibid.
[270] cf. Bragg, S. M. loc. cit. p. 7
[271] cf. ibid.
[272] cf. ibid.
[273] cf. Müller-Dauppert, B. ibid. p. 19
[274] cf. ibid.
[275] cf. ibid.

4.2.6 Dependency on the vendor

Special attention should be paid to the dependency factor. Hermes & Schwarz claim that in the short- and middle-run outsourcing decisions can be described as irreversible[276]. Outsourcing contract duration, however, usually accounts for several years and in addition to business processes transfer includes human resources and specific real assets[277]. All this results in interdependency of partners which again leads to certain risks[278]. If the service is very specific then it would be very difficult to change the vendor, and knowing that the present partner can significantly affect the relationship, it will be complicated to negotiate on the same level[279].

Thus, there are a number of serious risks to be factored into the decision to outsource a logistics function[280]. These risks can, in some cases, bring down the company or significantly worsen its competitive or financial position, and therefore they must be carefully weighed alongside numerous benefits of outsourcing[281].

---

[276] cf. Hermes, H. J. & Schwarz, G. loc. cit. p. 23
[277] cf. ibid.
[278] cf. ibid.
[279] cf. Engelbrecht, C. loc. cit. p. 22
[280] cf. Bragg, S. M. loc. cit. p. 8
[281] cf. ibid.

5. Planning Stage

The foregoing chapters were concerned with the key factors surrounding outsourcing projects with particular reference to its theoretical background. A large number of reasons was given that could form the basis for a decision to outsource a function. Also the risks were itemized to offset the reasons favouring outsourcing. This chapter will focus on the planning stage of an outsourcing project giving an overview of different steps towards transfer of logistics function to an external service provider. As with any significant new initiative, planning activities are very important. According to Kranke, the most fatal mistakes are made by the management during planning stages of the project and during transfer activities[282]. Therefore, the planning stage gained special attention in this work aiming at providing a solid understanding of the issues involved in outsourcing a logistics function.

5.1 Outsourcing Forms

Once a company has decided to move forward with assessing outsourcing, the management will need to identify the right form of outsourcing. Traditionally, outsourcing has focused on business *functions*[283]. But increasingly, the trend in outsourcing has been to broaden out services from pure business functions towards business *operations*[284]. Nowadays, it's been distinguished between several forms of outsourcing, and most of them are relevant in the context of logistics. Gericke, for example, differentiates between partial, complete and business process outsourcing[285].

---

282 cf. Kranke, A. loc. cit. p. 44
283 cf. Benn, I. & Pearcy, J. loc. cit. p. 42
284 cf. ibid. p. 43
285 cf. Gericke, J. (2005). Unterstützung von Logistik-Outsourcing-Entscheidngen in mittelständisch strukturierten Unternehmen. Taunusstein: Verlag Dr. H. H. Driesen GmbH. p. 76

Partial outsourcing (also called selective outsourcing or outtasking[286]) refers to transfer of a certain task within a function[287]. In this case the outsourcing partner is responsible only for implementation of this task, as for example, transportation and storage of certain type of goods[288]. Usually outtasking eliminates difficulties concerning personnel transfer (discussed in Chapter 3.3.2.5)[289]. This type of outsourcing sometimes serves as a substitute for collapsed complete outsourcing projects[290].

Another form is the so-called **complete** outsourcing (also referred to as total or strategic outsourcing)[291]. In this case the entire function is transferred to the service provider, as for example outsourcing of the whole warehousing facility[292]. That kind of project includes transfer of all resources and assignments within a function[293]. This form may cause the upper-mentioned dependency on the vendor[294].

Müller-Dauppert develops the total outsourcing concept and divides it into three sub forms: Total-Out, Total 3-Out and Total Invest-Out[295]:

1. **Total-Out**: transfer of logistics activities including all the premises on operating site without changing its location[296].
2. **Total 3-Out**: transfer of logistics activities to other site that belongs to the vendor; original premises therefore are used for other purposes, such as production or for sale[297].
3. **Total Invest-Out**: during transfer of logistics activities to the vendor, the production site is being handed over to an independent investor, who rents the facility out [298].

---

[286] cf. Mayer, A. G. & Söbbing, T. loc. cit. p. 26
[287] cf. Gericke, J. loc. cit; cf. Mayer, A. G. & Söbbing, T. ibid.
[288] cf. Gericke, J. ibid.
[289] cf. Mayer, A. G. & Söbbing, T. ibid.
[290] cf. ibid.
[291] cf. Gericke, J. ibid; cf. Mayer, A. G. & Söbbing, T. ibid.
[292] cf. ibid.
[293] cf. ibid.
[294] cf. Mayer, A. G. & Söbbing, T. ibid.
[295] cf. Müller-Dauppert, B. loc. cit. p. 26
[296] cf. ibid.
[297] cf. ibid.
[298] cf. ibid.

Another, more sophisticated form of outsourcing is the so-called **business process outsourcing (BPO)**[299]. BPO is the management of one or more specific business processes or functions by a third party, together with the IT that supports the process or function – and according to Halvey & Melby – is being perceived in the marketplace as the next generation of outsourcing[300]. In logistics, for example, the external service provider would assume control over entire distribution logistics of an outsourcer, including all connected processes and functions[301].
By all the upper-mentioned outsourcing alternatives the outsourcer has no or little control over transferred functions/tasks/processes. There is another additional outsourcing alternative by which the company can retain control: **the joint venture**[302]. Management decides for **joint venture** to eliminate potential tax burden arising from normal transfer alternatives, as well as to maintain certain level of control over the service transferred[303]. Normally, this initiative leads to the establishment of a legally independent entity (usually Ltd[304]), that functions according to cooperative contract (including Letter of Intent[305]) between the outsourcer and the vendor[306]. Both parties are aiming at achieving operative and strategic goals together, accordingly sharing losses and profits[307].

The research shows that in practice the majority of companies decide not for one certain form of outsourcing but for a unique combination of different

---

[299] cf. Gericke, J. loc. cit; cf. Mayer, A. G. & Söbbing, T. loc. cit. p. 29;
[300] cf. Halvey, J. K. & Melby, B. M. loc. cit. p. 1
[301] cf. Gericke, J. ibid.
[302] cf. Mayer, A. G. & Söbbing, T. ibid. p. 24; cf. Müller-Dauppert, B. loc. cit.
[303] cf. ibid.
[304] In English Law and other countries with similar laws a private limited company by shares (limited or Ltd.) is a type of limited company, with liability limited to the capital invested, i.e. by the sale of shares. In other words the shareholder's personal assets are protected in the event of bankruptcy but they will lose the capital invested in their shares. Source: en.wikipedia.org/wiki/Ltd
[305] The preferred vendor may push for the customer to enter into a letter of intent with the vendor which, at a minimum, sets out the general objectives of the parties. Vendors typically want to include a provision in the letter of intent that provides that the customer will enter into exclusive negotiations with the vendor for a certain number of days. Other common provisions include allocating costs and expenses, confidentiality obligations and more. Source: Halvey, J. K. & Melby, B. M. ibid.
[306] cf. Mayer, A. G. & Söbbing, T. ibid.
[307] cf. ibid.

approaches[308]. However, it is recommended to choose one form for outsourcing project and be consistent in its implication[309].

5.2 Identifying potential providers

After a company has decided on the right form (or combination of forms) of outsourcing, the management will need to identify the potential vendor or vendors that have the resources, capabilities, and requisite experience to provide the desired service[310]. Unless the decision to evaluate outsourcing has been kept confidential, the vendors will hear through an existing relationship with the customer or through the vendor's marketing that the company is considering outsourcing[311]. The organisation may already be targeted as a potential outsourcer[312]. However, even if the firm has an existing relationship with the vendor and thinks that in the long run this vendor is the right match for the company, the management should consider performing at least minimal due diligence[313] to see who else can provide similar services[314]. Such due diligence enables the outsourcing team to demonstrate that it has evaluated all of its alternatives with respect to the chosen vendor[315]. In case if the company has information about the vendors that it wants to target it is useful to draw up a long list, then, after doing due diligence on the vendors, shorten this list to the target vendor (typically between three and eight vendors)[316]. If the company is not familiar with all of the potential vendors, then it would be useful to:

- Obtain information from logistics reports/surveys
- Look at logistics publications

---

308 cf. Horchler, H. (1996). Outsourcing: Eine Analyse der Nutzung und ein Handbuch der Umsetzung. Köln: Datakontext-Fachverlag. p. 21
309 cf. ibid.
310 cf. Halvey, J. K. & Melby, B. M. loc. cit. p. 29
311 cf. ibid.
312 cf. ibid.
313 Due diligence – the process of reviewing and analysing in detail the capacity of a bidding organisation to meet future contract performance requirements. This may include a detailed assessment of the organisation's financial stability, legal risks, technical capacity and infrastructure. Source: http://www.vgpb.vic.gov.au/CA256C450016850B/0/073B1893942AC1C9CA256C5C0006AC1D
314 cf. Halvey, J. K. & Melby, B. M. ibid.
315 cf. ibid.
316 cf. ibid.

- Talk to other outsourcers[317].

In addition, Internet web pages may also be considered as another information source[318]. The following links are helpful in identifying potential logistics service providers in Germany:

- www.logismarket.de
- www.logistik-heute.de
- www.logistik-inside.de
- www.verkehrsrundschau.de
- www.dvz.de (Deutsche Verkehrs-Verlag)
- www.transportdata.de
- www.logistik-top100.de

Another source represents numerous associations that offer catalogues with information about their member companies[319]. Some of them are listed below:

- Bundesvereinigung Logistik e.V. (BVL)
- Bundesverband Materialwirtschaft, Einkauf und Logistik e.V. (BME)
- Bundesverband der Transportunternehmen e.V. (BVT)
- Bundesverband Güterkraftverkehr Logistik und Entsorgung e.V. (BGL)
- Deutschen Speditions- und Logistikverband e.V. (DSLV)[320].

There is a variety of ways to obtain lists of suppliers who can potentially enter into an outsourcing relationship with the company[321]. The company can encounter difficulties in finding potential suppliers only if it is located in a geographically isolated area, or if the service it demands is difficult to obtain so that there are no suppliers who can provide the service[322]. However, for the majority of a company's logistics functions, there are usually a number of suppliers nearby who can provide the service[323].

---

317 cf. Halvey, J. K. & Melby, B. M. loc. cit.
318 cf. Greaver, M. F. loc. cit. p. 172; cf. Müller-Dauppert, B. loc. cit. p. 34
319 cf. Müller-Dauppert, B. ibid.
320 cf. ibid.
321 cf. Bragg, S. M. loc. cit. p. 15
322 cf. ibid.
323 cf. ibid.

Greaver offers a list of examples of provider qualifications, summarized by hard and soft qualifications[324]. The hard qualifications are those that are primarily historically based and can be reasonably verified by due diligence[325]. The soft qualifications are more attitudinal, may or may not be verifiable, and could change based on the circumstances[326]:

Hard qualifications:	▪ Demonstrated ability to deliver today
	▪ Experience to deliver
	▪ Provider strengths
	▪ Superior performance
	▪ Deserved positive reputation
	▪ Proven customer satisfaction
	▪ Strong financial position
	▪ Proven management capabilities
	▪ Shared approach to problem solving
	▪ Strong transition experience
Soft Qualifications	▪ Trust, security, confidentiality
	▪ Positive attitude
	▪ Good chemistry
	▪ Good cultural fit
	▪ Clear vision of the market
	▪ Flexibility to change

The project team should consider whether this list is complete and add to it where appropriate[327]. Further, not all of these qualifications apply to each situation, and the project team should determine which should apply and which should be eliminated[328]. The reasons to outsource should help in reaching a conclusion about the necessary qualification criteria[329].

[324] cf. Greaver, M. F. loc. cit. p. 173
[325] cf. ibid.
[326] cf. ibid.
[327] cf. ibid. p. 174
[328] cf. ibid.
[329] cf. ibid.

5.3 Request for proposal

The core of the selection process is creating a request for proposal (RFP) and issuing it to suppliers, using a list of criteria to review the resulting supplier bids, and then checking the references of the best supplier candidates[330]. This process, as described in this part of the work, will result in the selection of a supplier.

Once a company has created a list of potential vendors, it should create a request for proposal document to send to each one[331]. However, in some cases companies decide early in the process that they are going to issue the RFP to only one vendor[332]. While this is generally not the recommended approach, it may make sense in situations where the company has a history with one particular vendor who is familiar with the customer's organisation[333]. There are, however, significant disadvantages of requesting a bid from only one vendor. The most obvious is that the outsourcer forfeits substantial negotiating leverage or that the vendor may be less flexible[334]. For most companies requesting multiple bids is the preferred approach because it may lead to competitive pricing or service levels and provide access to alternative solutions[335].

In order to ensure that the transfer of a function or a process will be accomplished without significant difficulties it is recommended to cover in RFP some of the issues which will be included in the future outsourcing contract[336]. The content of the outsourcing RFP varies greatly from outsourcer to outsourcer. For outsourcing of logistics services the following structure of RFP is advisable:

1. Objectives and scope of the project
2. Flow of material and quantity structure
3. Specification of services

[330] cf. Bragg, S. M. loc. cit. p. 15
[331] cf. ibid.
[332] cf. Halvey, J. K. & Melby, B. M. loc. cit. p. 31
[333] cf. ibid.
[334] cf. ibid.
[335] cf. ibid. p. 32
[336] cf. Müller-Dauppert, B. loc. cit. p. 34

4. Contractual aspects
5. Pricelists
6. Organisational issues[337].

Objectives and scope of the project: here the general terms of the project are described[338]. If the vendor is new to the company it is recommended to provide general description of the company, its existing services and short- and long-term goals[339]. By defining the scope, the number of potential suppliers willing to submit a bid may be reduced[340].

Flow of material and quantity structure: the description of material flow and quantity structure is required for quantifying of services and serves as a basis for price calculations[341].

Specification of services: provides a description of existing services and the services that the vendor will be required to offer[342]. It also lists those services not to be provided, if some parts of a function are being outsourced and other parts of it are being retained in-house[343]. This information is critical for the construction of adequate supplier bids[344].

Contractual aspects: this part is required to provide the vendor with an overview of legal and economic consequences derived from participating in the project[345]. Some of the key issues covered by the outsourcing contract are to be listed here, so that the vendor is able to asses potential risks derived from the relationship[346]. Some of the most important key points to be covered here are as follows: contract duration, transition issues, intellectual property, confidential information, pricing/fees, measuring performance, transfer of employees, transfer of assets, customer responsibilities, termination and more[347].

---

337 cf. Müller-Dauppert, B. loc. cit. p. 34
338 cf. ibid; cf. Halvey, J. K. & Melby, B. M. loc. cit. p. 32; cf. Bragg, S. M. loc. cit. p. 16
339 cf. Müller-Dauppert, B. ibid; cf. Halvey, J. K. & Melby, B. M. ibid.
340 cf. Bragg, S. M. ibid.
341 cf. Müller-Dauppert, B. ibid. p. 38
342 cf. ibid; cf. Halvey, J. K. & Melby, B. M. ibid.
343 cf. Bragg, S. M. ibid. p. 17
344 cf. ibid.
345 cf. Müller-Dauppert, B. ibid. p. 44
346 cf. ibid.
347 cf. Halvey, J. K. & Melby, B. M. ibid; cf. Müller-Dauppert, B. ibid.

Pricelists: the economics of outsourcing are complex and varied[348]. Agreements are typically based on either a fixed-price or cost-plus model[349]. In both of these models, the vendor sets a price for agreed-upon volume or services scope and charges additional fees for excess volume or services scope[350]. While it is almost certain that changes will occur and it is impossible to provide for every eventuality, a framework for the price adjustment mechanism should be well understood[351].

Organisational issues: organisational requirements should facilitate the process of communication between the outsourcer and the vendor[352]. The information flow mechanism should be developed, serving both parties of the project[353]. Especially helpful is the explanation of the selection process[354]. This may include a weighting of a number of criteria, such as a vendor's price, experience, financial stability, and references[355].

Most of the points above should be included in an RFP for any substantial outsourcing project. The mistake made by many companies is to spend too little time evaluating the bids submitted by outsourcing suppliers before selecting one[356]. The most common approach is to scan through the bids to look for the lowest price, and award the contract to that supplier[357]. That approach ignores the number of factors that should be researched prior to awarding a contract. The next section will give an insight into evaluating of proposals following by the vendor selection.

5.4 Selecting the vendor

Once final proposals are received from the vendors, the outsourcing team will need to review each of them and evaluate which vendor or vendors are best

[348] cf. Greaver, M. F. loc. cit. p. 192
[349] cf. ibid.
[350] cf. ibid.
[351] cf. ibid.
[352] cf. Müller-Dauppert, B. loc. cit.
[353] cf. ibid.
[354] cf. Bragg, S. M. loc. cit. p. 16
[355] cf. ibid.
[356] cf. ibid. p. 18
[357] cf. ibid.

suited to provide the desired services. The structure and scope of the vendor evaluation process vary depending on the customer's approach, the number of vendors being evaluated, time constraints, audit and report requirements[358]. Common steps of evaluation can include:

- Selecting key evaluation criteria
- Establishing a scoring system
- Weighting the key criteria
- Making final selection[359].

By the end of the evaluation period, the company should have identified a preferred vendor or vendors (depending on whether the customer elects to negotiate with one or more vendors).

5.4.1 Evaluation criteria

To facilitate the evaluation process, it is helpful to prepare a list of key criteria on which to judge the vendors and their proposals[360]. The items included on this list should reflect the customer's list of objectives for outsourcing. The types of criteria that a customer considers key will vary depending on the scope, value, and complexity of the proposed outsourcing transaction[361]. The following diagram on page 57 will give an overview of the most relevant examples of evaluation criteria[362].

Once the evaluation criteria are set by the company, the vendors should be ranked according to their fulfilment of the criteria.

5.4.2 Establishing a scoring system

Next, a scoring system should be established[363]. Each of the criteria should be assigned a score ranging from poor to outstanding[364]. A common and easy use

---

[358] cf. Halvey, J. K. & Melby, B. M. loc. cit. p. 36
[359] cf. ibid; Bruch, H. (1998). Outsourcing: Konzepte und Strategien, Chansen und Risiken. Wiesbaden: Verlag Gabler. pp. 150 *et. seq.*
[360] cf. ibid.
[361] cf. ibid.
[362] Based on the results of the research conducted by the Input Market Research Institute in 1995. Source: Bruch, H. ibid.
[363] cf. ibid.
[364] cf. ibid.

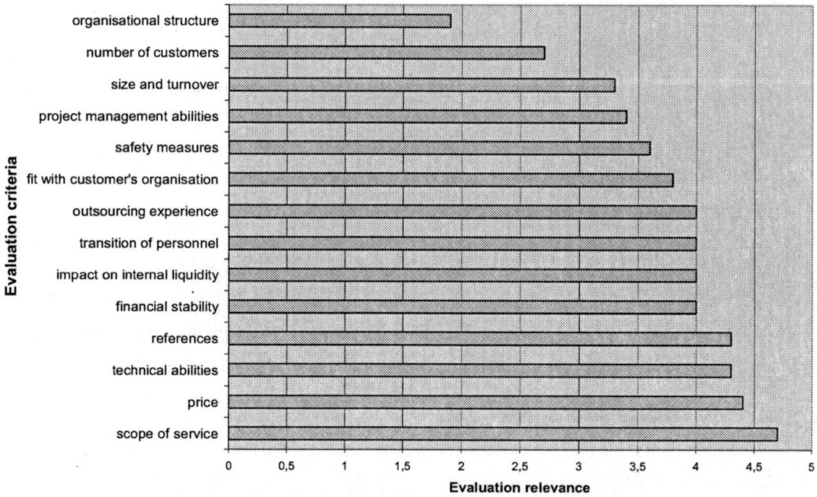

Diagram 11: Evaluation criteria for outsourcing vendor selection

scoring system is to rank the vendors in each category from 1 to 10, where 1 = poor, 5 = acceprable, and 10 = ooutstanding.

5.4.3 Weighting the key criteria

Not all evaluation criteria may be of equal importance. Customers engaging in more formal evaluation process should consider weighting each of the criteria to reflect the importance given to each[365]. A common approach for weighting the criteria is to assign a weight or percentage to each general category, with the total of all the weights equalling 100 per cent[366]. After the evaluation ballots have been filled out it needs to be tallied which will identify the top vendor or vendors[367].

5.4.4 Making final selection

Once the ballots have been tallied, the outsourcing team should take a final look at the top vendor or vendors. This can be done in a number of ways:

---

[365] cf. Bruch, H. loc. cit. p. 177
[366] cf. ibid.
[367] cf. ibid.

- An informal sign-off from the outsourcing team
- An informal sign-off from senior management
- A formal approval vote by the outsourcing team
- A formal letter of approval from senior management[368].

Some companies go so far as to have respondents who disagree with the top vendor or vendors to note the reasons for such disagreement[369].

Finally, the selection process can be very political. The outsourcing team should be aware that vendors may go around them and appeal to higher levels of management for favourable treatment, so that the team's selection may be voided and another supplier hired without their recommendation[370]. Although, it is not likely to happen, the outsourcing team should be aware of such problems in advance, so that they can be avoided[371].

This chapter gave an overview of the planning stage of an outsourcing project providing an insight into different forms of outsourcing, giving recommendations on the structure of Request for Proposal and reviewing the process of vendor selection. To sum up, it would be important to note that selecting a vendor based on the bid price is one of the least important factors – it is much more important, due to the long-term nature of the relationship, that the selection should be based on such factors as the operating style of the service provider, its compatibility with the company's staff, and its reputation for excellence.

---

[368] cf. Halvey, J. K. & Melby, B. M. loc. cit. p. 40
[369] cf. ibid.
[370] cf. Bragg, S. M. loc. cit. p. 24
[371] cf. ibid.

Conclusion

The practice of outsourcing logistics operations has grown significantly over the past few years. Research currently documents the high impact of outsourcing on the strategic evolution of enterprises. In an effort to concentrate on core competencies, to gain efficiency, and to improve services, companies are taking a close look at their logistics functions, assessing which activities might be better handled by an outside vendor. In many industries the pressure to achieve cost reductions and so to achieve greater competitiveness has been the primary reason for pursuing sophisticated and complex global agreements with third party service providers.

However, up to today, literature and logistics outsourcing research are lacking a more intensive discussion regarding the impact on a company's efficiency when certain functions are being outsourced, even though its beneficial importance is mentioned frequently. It is critical to understand the factors that may improve the efficiency:

Financially driven factors:

- Reduce investments in assets and allocate them to other projects
- Generate cash by transferring assets to the provider
- Reduce capital commitment

Cost-driven factors:

- Reduce costs through better provider performance / lower cost structure
- Turn fixed costs into variable costs

Yet, while there are many incentives to outsource a function and therefore increase the company's efficiency, there is also a number of risks related to this decision. These can range from minor pricing issues to non-performance by a supplier of the outsourced function. The company making the outsourcing decision must be aware of these risks when making the decision to hand over a function to a vendor.

If the company is aware of the potential pitfalls and is able to avoid them, then the savings achieved and efficiencies gained by outsourcing logistics activities can be enormous; but mismanaged planning initiatives will undoubtedly end in failure. The decision process for the outsourcing transaction is often a daunting task; a careful planning is often defined as the most important stage of the process. Management should definitely be concerned with the vendor selection procedure, since it is one of the critical success factors. If all the planning initiatives are accomplished properly in a sophisticated manner, then the benefits of using outsourcing will strongly outweigh the negatives.

To summarise, logistics outsourcing is a dynamic, shifting and growing business environment. There are advantages and disadvantages attached to outsourcing. If the process is properly managed and implemented, its advantages, in this work emphasised by the example of logistics functions, will outweigh its disadvantages, especially considering the key factor in Supply Chain Management: efficiency.

List of References

AMR Research (2005) "The Supply Chain Top 25" in Beschaffung Aktuell: Materialwirtschaft, Einkauf, Logistik. May, 2005.

Ballou, R. H. (1987). Basic Business Logistics. Englewood Cliffs: Prentice-Hall

Ballou, R. H. (1999). Business Logistics Management. Upper Saddle River: Prentice Hall

Ballou, R. H. (2004). Business Logistics/Supply Chain Management. Upper Saddle River: Pearson Prentice Hall

Benn, I. & Pearcy, J. (2002). Outsourcing: exploiting the skills of third parties. London: Hodder & Stoughton Educational

Black, J. (2003). A Dictionary of Economics, 2nd ed. Oxford: Oxford University Press

Bowersox, D. J. (1978). Logistical Management, 2nd ed. New York: Macmillian Publishing Company

Bowersox, D. J. et. al. (1986). Logistical Management, 3rd ed. New York: Macmillian Publishing Company

Bowersox, D. J. (1986). Third Party Partner – a timely concept. Columbus, Ohio: Ackerman

Bragg, S. M. (1998). Outsourcing. New York: John Wiley & Sons, Inc.

Bruch, H. (1998). Outsourcing: Konzepte und Strategien, Chansen und Risiken. Wiesbaden: Verlag Gabler

Bund, M. & Bendixen, B. (1998). Outsourcing von Logistikleistungen in Unternehmensentwicklung und Industrial Engineering Magazine. Vol. 47

Changsen, Z. (2005). Third Party Logistics Management. Berlin: Logos Verlag

Corsten, D. & Gabriel, C. (2004). Supply Chain Management erfolgreich umsetzen. Heidelberg: Physica-Verlag

Coyle, J. J. et. al. (1988). The management of Business Logistics, 4th ed. St. Paul, MN: West Publishing Company

De Kok, A. G. & Graves S. C. (eds). (2003). Supply Chain Management: Design, Coordination and Operation. Amsterdam: ElsevierB.V.

Dudek, F. & Weidt, S. (2004). Rahmendaten der Logistik. Fraunhofer IML / West LB

Engelbrecht, C. (2004). Logistikoptimierung durch Outsourcing. Wiebaden: Deutscher Universitäts-Verlag

Freiwald, S. (2005). Supply Chain Design. Frankfurt am Main: Peter Lang Verlag

Frost & Sullivan Consulting (2004). Junger Markt mit hohem Wachstumspotenzial in Marktbild Lager Magazine

Gericke, J. (2005). Unterstützung von Logistik-Outsourcing-Entscheidngen in mittelständisch strukturierten Unternehmen. Taunusstein: Verlag Dr. H. H. Driesen GmbH

Goold, M. & Luchs, K. S. (eds). (1996). Managing the Multibusiness Company: strategic issues for diversified groups. London: Routledge

Greaver, M. F. (1999). Strategic Outsourcing: A Structured Approach to Outsourcing Decisions and Initiatives. New York: AMACOM

Halvey, J. K. & Melby, B. M. (2000). Business Process Outsourcing: Process, Strategies, and Contracts. New York: John Wiley & Sons, Inc.

Hamel, G. & Prahalad, C. K. (1990). The Core Competence of the Corporation. Boston: Harvard Business Review

Hamel, G. & Prahalad, C. K. (1994). Competing for the Future. Boston: Harvard Business School Press

Handfield, R. B. & Nichols, E. L. (1999). Introduction to Supply Chain Management. Upper Saddle River: Prentice Hall

Heinrich, W. (ed). (1992). Outsourcing: Modelle-Strategien-Praxis. Bergheim: DATACOM Verlag

Heptner, K. (1999). Praxisbeispiele und Bewertung von Dienstleistern in Workshop "Logistik-Dienstleistungen Richtig Einkaufen". Mülheim an der Ruhr: Eiropäisches Transportforum

Hermes, H. J. & Schwarz, G. (eds). (2005). Outsourcing: Chansen und Risiken, Erfolgsfaktoren, rechtssichere Umsetzung. München: Haufe/Deloitte

Horngren, C. T. et. al. (2005). Introduction to management accounting, 14th ed. Upper Saddle River: Pearson/Prentice Hall

Jahn, H. C. et. al. (eds.) (2004). Sourcing. Frankfurt am Main: Frankfurter Allgemeine Buch

Köhler-Frost, W. (ed). (2005). Outsourcing: Schlüsselfaktoren der Kundenzufriedenheit. Berlin: Schmidt Verlag

Kranke, A. (2005a). Preis schlägt Service in Logistik Inside Magazine. Vol. 12/2005

Kranke, A. (2005b). Da muss jeder durch in Logistik Inside Magazine. Vol. 10/2005

Lambert, D. M. et. al. (1998). Supply Chain Management : Implementation Issues and Research Opportunities, in: The International Journal of Logistics Management, Vol. 9, No. 2

Lee, H. L. & Billington, C (1995). The Evolution of Supply Chain Management Models and Practice at Hewlett-Packard. Interfaces 25

Lee, H. L. & Ng, S. M. (1997). Introduction to the Special Issue on Global Supply Chain Management in Production and Operations Management, Vol. 5, No. 3

Lewis, C. (09/2003). Thinking outside the box in Logistics Europe Magazine

Mayer, A. G. & Söbbing, T. (2004). Outsourcing leicht gemacht. Frankfurt am Main: Redline Wirtschaft bei ueberreiter

Müller-Dauppert, B. (ed). (2005). Logistik-Outsourcing: Ausschreibung, Vergabe, Controlling. München: Verlag Heinrich Vogel

Murphy, P. R. & Woods, D. F. (2004). Contemporary Logistics, 8th ed. Upper Saddle River: Pearson Education

Pfohl, H. C. (ed). (2004). Erfolgsfaktor Kooperation in der Logistik. Berlin: Erich Smidt Verlag

Porter, M. (1985). Competitive Advantage: Creating and Sustaining Superior Performance. New York: The Free Press

Porter, M. (1999). Wettbewerb und Strategie. München: Econ

Schäfer-Kunz, J. & Tewald, C. (1998). Make-or-Buy-Entscheidungen in der Logistik. Wiesbaden: Deutscher Universitäts-Verlag

Schary, P .B. & Skjott-Larsen, T. (1998). Managing the Global Supply Chain. Copenhagen: Copenhagen Business School Press

Schary, P. B. & Skjott-Larsen, T. (2001). Managing the Global Supply Chain, 2nd Edition. Copenhagen: Copenhagen Business School Press

Scheja, K. & Jacob, P. (2005). Reibungslose Übergabe in Logistik Inside Magazine (10/2005)

Schönsleben, P. et. al. (2001). Nachhaltige Steigerung der Integration von Wertschöpfungsketten durch SCM. in: Supply Chain Management, I/2001

Schweiger, S. (2005). Gefahr droht immer in Beschaffung Aktuell Magazine April 2005

Seuring, S. (2003). Strategy and Organisation in Supply Chains. Heidelberg: Physica Verlag

Seuring, S. & Goldbach, M. (eds). (2002). Cost Management in Supply Chains. Heidelberg: Physica-Verlag

Taff, C. (1972). Management of Physical Distribution and Transportation, 5th ed. Homewood: Irwin

Weber, J. & Engelbrecht, C. (2002). In fremden Händen in Logistik Heute Magazine, 9/2002

Wißkirchen, F. (ed). (1999). Outsourcing – Projekte erfolgreich realisieren. Stuttgart: Schäffer-Poeschel Verlag

Internet Sources

Copacino, W. (1998). A growing tidal wave of supply-chain outsourcing. Retrieved on-line in the Internet on the 24th of April 2006: http://www.logisticsmgmt.com/article/CA145525.html?text=4pl

Eyefortransport (2006). Outsourcing Logistics 2006 Report. Retrieved on-line in the Internet on the 17th of May 2006

Foster, T. (1999). 4Pls: The next generation for supply chain outsourcing. Retrieved on-line in the Internet on the 21st of April 2006: http://www.logisticsmgmt.com/article/CA125187.html

Bibliography

Brindley, C. (ed). (2004). Supply Chain Risk. London: Ashgate Publishing

Eckel, C. (2005). International Trade, Flexible Manufacturing and Outsourcing. Göttingen: Center for Globalization and Europeanization of the Economy

Diehl, M. (1999). The Impact of International Outsourcing on the Skill Structure of Employment: Empirical Evidence from German Manufacturing Industries. Kiel: The Kiel Institute of World Economics

Göpfert, I. (2000). Logistik Führungskonzeption. München: Verlag Franz Vahlen

Gudehus, T. (2000). Logistik 1/2. Berlin: Springer

Hauschild, R. J. & Mansch, A. (1997). Erfahrungen aus der Bestandsaufnahme einer Auswahl von Outsourcingfällen für Logistik-Leistungen. Bremen: Institut für Weltwirtschaft und Internationales Management (IWIM)

Hodel, M. (1999). Outsourcing-Management: kompakt und verständlich. Wiesbaden: Vieweg Verlag

Horchler, H. (1996). Outsourcing: Eine Analyse der Nutzung und ein Handbuch der Umsetzung. Köln: Datakontext-Fachverlag

Jäntsch, E. & Schaberg, D. (2004). Managed Professional Outsourcing. Augsburg: Ubooks

Kleinert, J. (2000). Growing Trade in Intermediate Goods: Outsoucing, Global Sourcing or Increasing Importance of MNE Networks? Kiel: The Kiel Institute of World Economics

Köhler-Frost, W. (ed). (2000). Outsourcing: Eine strategische Allianz besonderen Typs. Berlin: Schmidt Verlag

Mol, M. J. (2001). Outsourcing, Supplier Relations and Internationalisation: Global Sourcing Strategy as a Chinese puzzle. Rotterdam: ERIM

Porter, M. E. (1980). Competitive Strategy: Techniques for Analyzing Industries and Competitors. New York: The Free Press

Reichert, C. (2005). Business Process Offshoring in the Indo-German Context. Bamberg: Difo-Druck GmbH

Scholtissek, S. (2004). New Outsourcing: die Dritte Revolution der Wertschöpfung in der Praxis. Berlin: Econ

Seifert, D. (2002). Collaborative Planning, Forecasting and Replenishment: how to create a Supply Chain Advantage. Bonn: Galileo Press

Weber, J. & Kummer, S. (1994). Logistik Management. Stuttgart: Schäffer-Poeschel Verlag

Appendices

§ 613a

Rechte und Pflichten bei Betriebsübergang[372]

(1) Geht ein Betrieb oder Betriebsteil durch Rechtsgeschäft auf einen anderen Inhaber über, so tritt dieser in die Rechte und Pflichten aus den im Zeitpunkt des Übergangs bestehenden Arbeitsverhältnissen ein. Sind diese Rechte und Pflichten durch Rechtsnormen eines Tarifvertrags oder durch eine Betriebsvereinbarung geregelt, so werden sie Inhalt des Arbeitsverhältnisses zwischen dem neuen Inhaber und dem Arbeitnehmer und dürfen nicht vor Ablauf eines Jahres nach dem Zeitpunkt des Übergangs zum Nachteil des Arbeitnehmers geändert werden. Satz 2 gilt nicht, wenn die Rechte und Pflichten bei dem neuen Inhaber durch Rechtsnormen eines anderen Tarifvertrags oder durch eine andere Betriebsvereinbarung geregelt werden. Vor Ablauf der Frist nach Satz 2 können die Rechte und Pflichten geändert werden, wenn der Tarifvertrag oder die Betriebsvereinbarung nicht mehr gilt oder bei fehlender beiderseitiger Tarifgebundenheit im Geltungsbereich eines anderen Tarifvertrags dessen Anwendung zwischen dem neuen Inhaber und dem Arbeitnehmer vereinbart wird.

(2) Der bisherige Arbeitgeber haftet neben dem neuen Inhaber für Verpflichtungen nach Absatz 1, soweit sie vor dem Zeitpunkt des Übergangs entstanden sind und vor Ablauf von einem Jahr nach diesem Zeitpunkt fällig werden, als Gesamtschuldner. Werden solche Verpflichtungen nach dem Zeitpunkt des Übergangs fällig, so haftet der bisherige Arbeitgeber für sie jedoch nur in dem Umfang, der dem im Zeitpunkt des Übergangs abgelaufenen Teil ihres Bemessungszeitraums entspricht.

---

[372] Source: BGB

(3) Absatz 2 gilt nicht, wenn eine juristische Person oder eine Personenhandelsgesellschaft durch Umwandlung erlischt.

(4) Die Kündigung des Arbeitsverhältnisses eines Arbeitnehmers durch den bisherigen Arbeitgeber oder durch den neuen Inhaber wegen des Übergangs eines Betriebs oder eines Betriebsteils ist unwirksam. Das Recht zur Kündigung des Arbeitsverhältnisses aus anderen Gründen bleibt unberührt.

(5) Der bisherige Arbeitgeber oder der neue Inhaber hat die von einem Übergang betroffenen Arbeitnehmer vor dem Übergang in Textform zu unterrichten über:

1. den Zeitpunkt oder den geplanten Zeitpunkt des Übergangs,
2. den Grund für den Übergang,
3. die rechtlichen, wirtschaftlichen und sozialen Folgen des Übergangs für die Arbeitnehmer und
4. die hinsichtlich der Arbeitnehmer in Aussicht genommenen Maßnahmen.

(6) Der Arbeitnehmer kann dem Übergang des Arbeitsverhältnisses innerhalb eines Monats nach Zugang der Unterrichtung nach Absatz 5 schriftlich widersprechen. Der Widerspruch kann gegenüber dem bisherigen Arbeitgeber oder dem neuen Inhaber erklärt werden.

Jayasimha, K. R. (2002). Logistics Management – An Introduction. Retrieved on-line in the Internet on the 21st of April 2006: http://www.icfaipress.org/books/Logistics%20management% 20-%20Vol-1.asp

McGill, D. (2004). Building a High Performance Business Model. Retrieved on-line in the Internet: http://www.accenture.com/Global/Services/By_Industry/Media_and_Entertainment/R_and_I/HighTools.htm

The Supply Chain Top 25[373]

	Company	Ranking according to AMR Research
1.	Dell	20,75
2.	Nokia	13,31
3.	Procter & Gamble	11,70
4.	IBM	11,31
5.	Wal-Mart Stores	11,27
6.	Toyota Motor	11,08
7.	Johnson & Johnson	10,93
8.	Johnson Controls	10,70
9.	Tesco	9,43
10.	PersiCo	9,10
11.	Nissan Motor	9,09
12.	Woolworths	8,80
13.	Hewlett-Packard	8,30
14.	3M	8,09
15.	GlaxoSmithKline	7,95
16.	POSCO	7,85
17.	Coca Cola	7,65
18.	Best Buy	7,53
19.	Intel	7,47
20.	Anheuser Busch	7,45
21.	The Home Depot	7,29
22.	Lowe's	7,00
23.	L'Oreal	6,98
24.	Canon	6,94
25.	Marks & Spencer	6,89

[373] According to AMR Research Report "The Supply Chain Top 25" in Beschaffung Aktuell: Materialwirtschaft, Einkauf, Logistik (05/2005). p. 10